THE STORY OF A LIFE

THE STORY
OF A LIFE

Memoirs of a Young Jewish Woman
in the Russian Empire

Anna Pavlovna Vygodskaia

TRANSLATED AND EDITED BY

Eugene M. Avrutin and Robert H. Greene

NIU PRESS
DeKalb, Illinois

© 2012 by Northern Illinois University

Published by the Northern Illinois University Press, DeKalb, Illinois 60115

All Rights Reserved

Design by Shaun Allshouse

Library of Congress Cataloging-in-Publication Data

Vygodskaia, Anna Pavlovna, b. 1868.

[Istoriia odnoi zhizni. English]

The story of a life : memoirs of a young Jewish woman in the Russian Empire
/ Anna Pavlovna Vygodskaia ; edited and translated by Eugene M. Avrutin and
Robert H. Greene.

p. cm.

Includes bibliographical references and index.

ISBN 978-0-87580-671-6 (pbk.: acid-free paper) —

ISBN 978-1-60909-046-3 (electronic)

1. Vygodskaia, Anna Pavlovna, b. 1868—Childhood and youth.
2. Jews—Belarus—Babruisk—Biography. 3. Jews—Belarus—Babruisk—
Social life and customs. 4. Jews—Education—Russia—History—19th century—
Sources. 5. Jews—Cultural assimilation—Russia—History—19th century—
Sources. 6. Babruisk (Belarus)—Biography. I. Avrutin,
Eugene M. II. Greene, Robert H., 1975- III. Title.

DS135.B383V94913 2012

305.892'404721092—dc23

[B]

2011034642

Contents

Acknowledgments

We would like to thank all the individuals and institutions that helped support a project that has been several years in the making. The Program in Jewish Culture and Society at the University of Illinois, the Hadassah-Brandeis Institute, and the Woodrow Wilson International Center for Scholars offered generous financial support. Vadim Jigoulov, Misha Krutikov, Michael Makin, Natan Meir, Brian Porter-Szücs, Clint Walker, and Christine Worobec provided valuable assistance with questions of translation and context. Ellen Kellman, Antony Polonsky, and Barbara Alpern Engel helped track down obscure references and names. Agnieszka Jagodińska and Anna Cichopek translated the Polish passages. Amy Alspaugh provided research assistance at the Woodrow Wilson Institute and the Library of Congress. Our editor, Amy Farranto, has been of tremendous help and support. Special thanks also to Barbara Engel, Anya Jabour, and Ted Weeks, who offered numerous constructive comments, and saved us from several infelicities of phrasing and glaring omissions. Any errors or lapses of style that remain are ours alone.

For consistency's sake, we have retained Vygodskaia's Russian spelling for place names from the former Russian Empire that are in present-day Belarus, Lithuania, Poland, Russia, and Ukraine. We have followed a modified Library of Congress transliteration system for Cyrillic that omits the final diacritical mark for place names (thus Kazan, not Kazan'), and the YIVO transliteration system for Yiddish. The names of certain figures in the text are presented in the form most familiar to English-language readers (thus Dubnow and Tchaikovsky).

Pale of Settlement, 1850. Map drawn by Merrily Shaw of the Russian, East European, and Eurasian Center at the University of Illinois.

Introduction

Eugene M. Avrutin and Robert H. Greene

In the mid-1930s, the renowned Jewish historian Simon Dubnow[1] encouraged Jewish educator Anna Pavlovna Vygodskaia (1868–1943) to write an autobiography about her experiences in prerevolutionary Russia. Initially, Vygodskaia was reluctant to take up Dubnow's offer, fearing that her "ordinary life experiences" would be of little interest to the reading public. Yet in the end Dubnow's entreaties prevailed, and the first volume appeared in Riga in 1938 to considerable acclaim.[2] One reviewer, writing for the Russian émigré newspaper *Segodnia*, observed that Vygodskaia's recollections "are imbued with tender warmth" and faithfully and simply recount life as it was half a century before.[3] In his preface to the autobiography, Dubnow recognized that Vygodskaia illuminated "all of the minor little details [of everyday life] to which male memoirists usually pay no heed, but which are so very important for the history of our material culture and national traditions." Despite Vygodskaia's initial reservations, *Istoriia odnoi zhizni* (The Story of a Life) is an extraordinary and rare historical document of Jewish childhood and young adult life in Tsarist Russia that has yet to receive the readership that it deserves.[4]

The Story of a Life draws on a number of popular autobiographical genres—it is styled as a family chronicle, a childhood and school autobiography, and a first-person narrative of social integration.[5] While several East European Jewish women's memoirs have been translated and published in recent years, *The Story of a Life* is one of only a handful written in Russian by a Jewish woman, and is the only first-person narrative to describe the unprecedented social opportunities, as well as the many political and personal challenges, that young Jewish women and men experienced in the 1870s and 1880s.[6] In her young adult life, Anna Vygodskaia was not drawn to revolutionary Jewish politics or tempted by the allure of emigration but instead sought to integrate herself into an emerging civil society.[7] Vygodskaia situates Jewish assimilation—the gradual transformation of Jewish religious practices, culture, and learning; the abandonment of external markers of Jewishness; and participation in Russian culture, society, and institutions—against the backdrop of profound socioeconomic and intellectual changes that took place in the second half of the nineteenth century. At a time when the vast majority of Russia's Jews continued to reside in small market towns in the Pale of Settlement, Vygodskaia liberated herself from the world of the Pale and immersed herself in the day-to-day rhythms, educational activities, and new intellectual opportunities in the imperial capital. Unlike most Jewish women (and men) in the Russian Empire, Vygodskaia was educated in Russian schools, spoke and read Russian fluently, pursued and obtained higher education in the capital, and traveled frequently to, from, and around St. Petersburg.

Until recently, the reconstruction of Jewish women's lives, in all of their geographic diversity and social complexity, has been virtually absent from most historical narratives and interpretations of East European Jewish culture and society. The marginalization of Jewish women's history can be explained in part by the traditional preoccupation of scholarship with the history of ideas and mass politics, and in part by the closure of the archives.[8] Since the breakup of the Soviet Union in 1991, scholars have used court records, police reports, letters and petitions, and many other personal papers generated, recorded, and preserved by the state to produce methodologically groundbreaking studies of the Jewish family and the gendered construction of everyday experiences. Nevertheless, even with the outpouring of new archival materials, a critical assessment of the life stories of women, whose own personal archives were either fragmentary or, in most cases, nonexistent, remains a complicated task for the historian.[9]

Reconstructing Anna Vygodskaia's life story produces numerous methodological challenges. To the best of our knowledge, her papers were not preserved in an archive, and her biography remains highly fragmentary and difficult to piece together. Yet Vygodskaia's life and work were not entirely erased from the historical record. Traces of her activities appear, however fleetingly, in contemporary memoirs and diaries, official administrative records, newspaper articles, and pamphlets by and about her, and in an all too brief biographical entry in a memorial book of Jewish teachers.[10] As is the case with so many first-person narratives written years after the events recounted, Vygodskaia's recollections are filled with intentional omissions, lapses in memory, and accidental distortions, to say nothing of editorial alterations.[11] But even if we take into account the documentary limitations of the memoir, Vygodskaia's life story offers a unique glimpse of Jewish daily life that rarely appears in public sources: neighborly interactions, children's games and household rituals, love affairs and emotional outbursts, clothing customs and leisure activities. While most first-person narratives reconstruct a Jewish world that is isolated and self-contained, *The Story of a Life* is remarkable for its depiction of vibrant and dynamic encounters in a multiethnic and multiconfessional imperial community. Anna Vygodskaia describes the changing Jewish world she grew up in and later abandoned. She also relates the various everyday encounters between Jewish parents and young, ambitious children anxious to leave the world of the Pale; Polish teachers and schoolchildren; and Russian students, professors, and imperial administrators.

Anna's World in the Pale

The Russian government mandated that all imperial subjects carry an internal passport when traveling beyond their permanent place of residence. The vast majority of the empire's Jewish population, acquired as a result of the partitions of Poland-Lithuania (1772, 1793, 1795), faced additional restrictions that prohibited them from taking up permanent residence in the interior provinces of the empire and required them to remain within the so-called Pale of Settlement. The Pale stretched along the western borderlands of the Russian Empire, encompassing much of present-day Lithuania, Poland, Belarus, Moldova, Ukraine, and western Russia. During the Great Reform era (1855–81), Alexander II issued several significant edicts that made Jewish residence restrictions less burdensome and helped facilitate the integration of select "useful" Jews in Russian civil society. Merchants of the first and second guilds (like Anna's father), select artisans, students, and army veterans obtained the privilege to travel and reside outside the boundaries of the Pale of Settlement. But until the Revolution of 1917, in spite of the state's relaxation of restrictions on mobility, Jews continued to encounter a set of convoluted and at times contradictory laws governing where they could move and how long they could travel within and beyond the Pale.[12]

Anna Pavlovna Vygodskaia, née Paperna, was born in 1868 and spent the first years of her life in Bobruisk, a mid-sized border town located in Minsk province in the very heart of the Pale of Settlement. Situated on the Berezina River and at the intersection of trade routes connected to some of the most prosperous commercial centers in the southwestern region of the Russian Empire, the town attracted small-scale merchants and skilled craftsmen who traded or exported timber, dry goods, and grain.[13] In the nineteenth century, Bobruisk's population comprised a diverse mixture of Poles, Belorussians, ethnic Russians, and a disproportionately high (and growing) number of Jews. In 1804, only 504 Jews were counted as permanent residents of Bobruisk. But by the time the Russian government conducted the 1897 census, the Jewish population had grown to 20,700, accounting for approximately 60 percent of the town's residents.[14] The Jewish community, however, was not a homogeneous one. Both the Hasidim and the Mitnagdim had established a firm social base in Bobruisk. While the Hasidim engaged in lengthy and ecstatic prayers and insisted that all people could attain mystical union with the Creator, the Mitnagdim followed rabbinical authority, arguing that salvation would come only through legitimate Torah study. Even as they quarreled among themselves, both groups struggled to suppress the rising challenge of new ideas associated with the Haskalah (the Jewish Enlightenment) and economic modernization.[15]

An imperial official working for the Minsk provincial statistical committee left a rather unflattering description of Bobruisk at the end of the nineteenth century: "After crossing the fortress, you see a row of paltry, tiny homes that stand on filthy, smelly streets. All summer long, the mud brings much luxury and freedom to the pigs who, together with other 'noble' animals, roam the streets by the dozens."[16] For Vygodskaia, the pigs were less a problem than the people. She remembered Bobruisk as a sleepy provincial town whose inhabitants "sealed themselves off from the rest of the world. . . . Half a century would pass before one could discern any development or growth in towns such as Bobruisk." In the 1870s, however, the face of the muddy provincial town did begin to change as many towns and cities in the northwest region of the empire experienced the growing pains of economic modernization. The railroad, which connected Bobruisk to Minsk, Vil'na, Gomel, and the port city of Libava, as well as destinations beyond the Pale, came to play an important role in the cultural and economic life of the town. After 1873, Bobruisk merchants relied on the Libava-Romensk railway line to distribute lumber more efficiently and cost-effectively by eliminating overhead expenses associated with water transport.[17] In Bobruisk, as in so many other places in the western borderlands, the last three decades of the nineteenth century witnessed also the emergence of a host of new cultural, educational, and political institutions. By exposing more and more people to secular ideas and to the latest fashions and social customs of the day, voluntary associations and government-sponsored schools helped transform public life and destabilize communal authority.[18]

Though the railroad had come and their numbers had grown, the vast majority of Bobruisk Jews continued to live their daily lives in economic poverty, working as shopkeepers, day laborers, street peddlers, and skilled artisans. Anna, however, came from a more respectable milieu. The Papernas were a prominent, pious, and learned Mitnagdic family that had resided in Bobruisk for more than five generations. According to family lore, her father's great-great-grandfather Isroel-Levin had ties to wealthy Polish magnates and reportedly married seven different women, each of whom bore him children. Isroel-Levin saw to it that his sons and daughters married into some of the most respected Jewish families in Lithuania, Poland, and Galicia. But because Isroel-Levin divided the inheritance among his many children, the family fortune dried up as quickly as it had been acquired.

Anna's grandfather Isroel Paperna had been married off to the daughter of a pious rabbi from Kopyl (a small town some 140 kilometers east of Bobruisk). Isroel, however, was drawn more to the comforts of life than to Talmudic learning. Vygodskaia remembered him as a dandy with a penchant for elegant pipes, fancy dress, and fine furniture. Ever restless, Isroel managed to stay in Kopyl for only three years—long enough to father two children: the prominent man of letters Avraam, and Anna's father, Faitel'. Thanks to a family connection, Isroel found work with the wealthy industrialist Isaak Zabludovskii, who owned a lumber factory in Belostok, and thus appeared at home infrequently, usually only for the high holidays. A third son, the educator Grigorii, was born after Isroel had begun to make his business trips to Belostok.[19]

In his own autobiographical reflections, Anna's Uncle Avraam recalled that Isroel's commercial encounters had infused the Paperna family with a "new spirit" and succeeded in "stirring up" life in the sleepy town of Kopyl. While working in the lumber industry, Isroel not only associated with people of progressive leanings but also made occasional trips across the border to Germany. Here he encountered Jews who differed from their coreligionists to the east in dress, speech patterns, and religious practices, and even developed personal attachments outside the Jewish community.[20] Over the course of eighteen years of traveling back and forth across the border, Isroel changed his views on many aspects of Jewish life. Avraam Paperna recalled one moment that made an especially memorable impression upon the Paperna family and their inquisitive neighbors. Isroel had just arrived back in Kopyl from a business trip on the eve of Yom Kippur. When he stepped out of his carriage wearing a fashionable short frock coat and long pants, with his beard neatly trimmed and his long blond hair tied back, the Jews of Kopyl, clad in modest black with their beards unshorn, could not believe their eyes. "The Jewish community," Avraam drily noted in his autobiography, "remembered this particular Yom Kippur for a long time." Isroel commuted regularly between Kopyl and Belostok until he lost his position in the lumber factory, at which time he decided to relocate the entire family to Bobruisk.[21]

Despite extreme social and family pressures (one of Isroel's cousins was the most distinguished Mitnagdic rabbi in Bobruisk), Isroel and his three sons represented a small but growing number of Bobruisk Jews who were drawn to the forbidden.[22] Anna's father, Faitel', was perhaps the most "assimilated" of the Paperna brothers. Anna notes that the education her father had received in the *heder*, or elementary school in the East European Jewish community, had given him a solid background in sacred texts and religious subjects but had not prepared him for a career in the world. Unable to find suitable employment in Bobruisk, Faitel' followed in the footsteps of his father and relied on his wife's family connections to land a job, securing an unspecified position in the Siberian gold mines. When Anna was only two years old, her father left the family to live and work in a "purely Russian environment" at the opposite end of the empire.[23] Ten years spent in Siberia left their mark on Faitel's appearance and consciousness, and it was there that Faitel' changed his name to the more suitably Russian-sounding Pavel Semënovich. Anna's uncles, Avraam and Grigorii, defied conventional expectations as well by choosing to enroll in the new state-sponsored teachers' seminaries in Vil'na and Zhitomir, where they studied a traditional Jewish curriculum supplemented by secular subjects. Avraam and Grigorii represented the first generation of Russian Jewish intellectuals who were proficient in the Russian language and felt at home in Russian elite culture.[24] According to Anna, Grigorii was also responsible for piquing her mother's interest in secular knowledge, and after he left to study in Vil'na, Anna's mother hired a tutor to continue her lessons in arithmetic, Russian literature, and other secular subjects. In a conservative environment, where boys were supposed to fulfill their religious vocation by acquiring proficiency in sacred texts in the heder and then, if gifted, in a yeshiva, and where girls lacked any institutionalized framework of education, the Paperna family's behavior proved exceptional and was the talk of a gossipy provincial town.[25]

Anna was still a young girl when her mother died of tuberculosis at the age of twenty-six. Anna and her older sister moved from one relative to another, while their father continued to work in the Siberian gold mines. At first, the girls remained in Bobruisk with their grandfather Isroel and his wife, a formidable woman whose eccentricities provided Anna with much fodder for her memoirs. After a year, Faitel' sent word from Siberia that his daughters should go live with their Uncle Grigorii, who taught in a public elementary school in Zakrochim (in Polish, Zakroczym), a small town in Russian Poland near Warsaw, about 720 kilometers west of Bobruisk. Here, Vygodskaia attended a public school for girls, where she was taught in Polish, even though the imperial government's educational policies of the time stipulated that Russian was the official language of instruction.[26] In this small border town neither ethnic differences nor religious customs seemed to create impermeable boundaries between neighbors. "Our life in Zakrochim," Vygodskaia recalled, "passed quietly, without any great disturbances. Jews, Poles, and some Russians too lived together peacefully here, side by side." Unlike state-generated documents (most of which capture male voices and tell us precious little about people's feelings, attitudes, or prejudices), Vygodskaia's writing recalls the intimate social universe that Jews and their Christian neighbors shared and inhabited.[27]

After three years in Zakrochim, the sisters relocated westward once again, this time to Plotsk (in Polish, Płock), where they stayed with their Uncle Avraam, a teacher in the town's secondary school, or gymnasium, which prepared students for higher education. Vygodskaia had grown up speaking Yiddish and studied Polish in the gymnasium, but it was Avraam who instilled in her a special love for all things Russian and a thirst for knowledge. Avraam Paperna, like so many other radical Haskalah literary critics in the era of the Great Reforms, felt that a mastery of the Russian language would ultimately reward the Jewish people with civil integration and equal rights and privileges in imperial society. As Avraam saw it, the archaic Hebrew language could have "an effect on but the few," whereas Yiddish might serve as a conduit for instructing the entire Jewish nation and ultimately arousing "a love for the national tongue [Russian]."[28] In his published writings, Avraam argued extensively in favor of women's education as well. Drawing on the ideas of the prominent pedagogue, scientist, and man of letters Nikolai Pirogov, and condemning those conservative critics who felt that women should be denied access to knowledge, Avraam believed that the education of women would benefit society as a whole.[29]

Anna was around twelve or thirteen years old when her father returned from Siberia. She and her sister went to live with him and his new wife in Vil'na, a multiethnic city known by multiple names to its various inhabitants (Wilno in Polish, Vilne in Yiddish, and Vilnius in Lithuanian). By the end of the nineteenth century, Vil'na was home to nearly sixty-three thousand Jews, approximately 41 percent of the city's population."[30] Anna spent her formative years here, in the very heart of Jewish life and culture, but as she recalls in her autobiography, she came to feel smothered by cultural traditions and middle-class conventions that were out of step with her "desire for a better life, the striving toward what is good, toward self-improvement." Already as a teenager, Anna came to see education as the key to achieving the kind of life she so desired. As part of its deeply rooted heritage, however, the East European Jewish community placed little value on the education of Jewish girls, promoting religious textual learning for males while actively restricting females from sacred study. Nevertheless, as a result of the gendered divisions that had structured Jewish society for several centuries, young Jewish women benefited from what the cultural critic Iris Parush has called their "marginality." While most girls did not receive a formal religious education, they could read secular literature, as well as ethical and mystical texts, in the Yiddish language and thus, in the nineteenth century, were able to immerse themselves in modern secular culture to a far greater degree than their male counterparts.[31] Anna, though, desired more than private study and the rudiments of a secular education. Fortunately for her, at this very time the choices available to and paths taken by Jewish women were being radically transformed.[32] By the 1870s and 1880s, private schools, gymnasia, and trade schools financed by a network of Jewish philanthropic organizations, as well as new institutions in the imperial capital, such as the Women's Medical Courses and the Higher Women's Courses, offered women unprecedented opportunities for social and geographic mobility, while opening up new paths of employment in the fields of medicine and teaching—two arenas that the autocratic regime deemed appropriate for women's participation.[33] Anna longed to be a part of this wider world and dreamed of attending the Higher Women's Courses in St. Petersburg.

With the passing of the older generation, Anna's family had grown more lax in their religious devotions and more acculturated in manners of dress, speech, education, and mores. Yet however receptive Anna's father and stepmother may have been to their daughter's secular studies, they nonetheless opposed her decision to pursue higher education. For an increasingly prosperous family like the Papernas (Faitel's financial success eventually earned him the distinguished status of a merchant of the first guild), the cost of tuition was not a major obstacle; rather, it was a fear that their unmarried daughter's decision to leave home and study in the capital would damage the family's carefully cultivated aura of middle-class respectability. "You can study anything you want and take lessons from the best teachers in Vil'na," Anna recalled her stepmother pleading with her, "but stay home, don't disgrace our family." To pursue her studies in St. Petersburg, Anna needed more than her family's blessing; she required her father's written permission. Until 1914, imperial law prevented an unmarried woman from traveling without her father's consent (a married woman required her husband's permission).[34]

Though she had overcome (or circumvented) the bureaucratic obstacles of Russian imperial officialdom and had been admitted to the Higher Women's Courses, Anna waited two months for her father to sign the necessary travel documents. Unlike many other women who found themselves in similar situations, Anna did not threaten to convert to Christianity, nor did she arrange a "fictitious marriage" with a progressive young man (two popular strategies that would have given her the automatic right to leave her parents' home and reside in the imperial capital).[35] In the end, Vygodskaia disobeyed her father's wishes and traveled to St. Petersburg without obtaining his signature. After arriving in the imperial capital, she wrote home, at her cousin's suggestion, saying that, unless her father sent along the requisite paperwork, she would enroll in the midwifery courses, which, through a bureaucratic oversight, enrolled Jews freely and granted students legal residency rights in the capital. Faced with the potential shame of having a daughter who was a midwife, Faitel' eventually conceded and signed the documents. This clever bit of blackmail did not seem to have damaged Anna's relations with her family. While studying in the capital, she traveled home for winter holidays and the summer recess and received a monthly allowance from her family sufficient to cover her room and board and excursions to the theater and opera.

During Anna's years in St. Petersburg (1885–89), police routinely targeted, harassed, and expelled large number of Jews from the imperial capital because their residency papers and other legal documents were not in proper order, yet Anna experienced no problems with the law.[36] By 1886, despite official impediments to their mobility and the rise of ethnic tensions, the number of Jewish men and women enrolled in universities and special women's educational institutions had increased a hundredfold since 1840. Although Jews accounted for just over 4 percent of the empire's population, Jewish women made up an astonishingly high 17 percent of Anna's classmates at the Higher Women's Courses.[37] Yet even as Anna developed close friendships with other male and female students from the Pale, she rushed to immerse herself in the wider, secular world of the capital— exploring the neighborhoods of St. Petersburg, learning to navigate the streetcars and crowded boulevards, scrambling for discounted tickets to the opera, joining reading circles and study groups, and living the life of a young woman free for the first time to set her own path in life.

"My Beloved Courses"

Anna came of age at a time when educated Russian society and the imperial regime alike weighed in on the so-called women's question, contesting the public role, civic rights, and legal status of women in the Russian Empire. A key aspect of the debates centered around the issue of women's access to higher education. Supporters such as Anna's Uncle Avraam maintained that qualified women should be guaranteed the same educational opportunities as their male counterparts. Couching their arguments in well-intentioned if patriarchal tones, some proponents claimed that well-educated women would make better mothers and citizens. By contrast, conservatives and chauvinists argued that the feminine temperament was unsuited for such intellectual rigors, and that women's presence in university lecture halls and laboratories would lead to a dilution of standards and serve as a distracting temptation for industrious male students.[38] Although Alexander II's University Statute of 1863 formally banned women from enrolling at universities in the empire, the regime recognized the need for trained female teachers and medical personnel and was reluctant to drive them abroad in search of an education. In 1876, the emperor granted permission for special women's schools to be established in St. Petersburg, Moscow, Kiev, and Kazan. The most celebrated of these was the Higher Women's Courses in St. Petersburg, popularly known as the Bestuzhev Courses, after their first director, the eminent historian Konstantin Bestuzhev-Riumin. Founded in 1878, enrollment was open to women of all social and religious backgrounds, although young women from gentry families predominated in the early years. Subsidies from the Ministry of Education and the St. Petersburg City Duma were insufficient to maintain operation, and the administration relied on tuition revenue and generous support from sympathetic donors (including the Gintsburg family, the renowned Russian Jewish financiers, communal activists, and philanthropists).[39]

By the time Anna matriculated in 1885, the Bestuzhev Courses had expanded to a four-year program, boasting a new building of its own, state-of-the-art laboratories, and a full range of academic offerings taught by a distinguished faculty drawn from the best institutions in the capital. Students had the option of enrolling in the historical-philological faculty, which offered a classical liberal arts education, or of pursuing a course of study that emphasized the natural and applied sciences. Vygodskaia recalls that "like the majority of female students," she opted for the latter—"such was the general mood of the times." The popularity of scientific study among Russian youth in Anna's day not only was a function of general interest in the explanatory power of science but also reflected a confidence that mastering medicine, botany, chemistry, and agronomy could achieve practical benefits in society at large.[40] Unlike their male counterparts, for whom a university degree meant increased employment opportunities and access to promotion in the civil service, women who completed the Bestuzhev Courses and other special women's institutes of higher learning struggled to find a place for themselves in imperial society. Many emigrated, to continue their studies abroad. Others pursued further medical training to become nurses, doctors, or specialists. The majority, like Anna herself, sought to make a contribution to society by becoming teachers, headmistresses, and private tutors. Historian Christine Ruane calculates that of the 1,346 women who completed the Bestuzhev Courses between 1882 and 1896, more than 71 percent became teachers.[41]

Though law and tradition restricted Russian women from entry into government service and most professions, higher education did change the way that female students thought about themselves and their relationship to the wider world. Women enrolled at the Courses referred to themselves as *kursistki*, and Vygodskaia uses this term throughout the memoir to describe herself and her classmates. A strong sense of corporate identity and solidarity emerged among the kursistki, who not only busied themselves with coursework but also staffed the student cafeteria, formed delegations to present grievances to the faculty, and represented the Courses at social and civic functions in the capital. If the police arrested a female student on suspicion of revolutionary activity—a not infrequent occurrence in the reign of Alexander III—her fellow kursistki banded together to work toward securing her release and gathering packages to make her jail time less miserable. Vygodskaia recalls, "Each of us felt responsible for everything that took place within the institution's walls, and the honor of our Courses was dear to our hearts." Historian Susan K. Morrisey describes this sense of student solidarity, or *studenchestvo*, as "a unique and plastic ethos, which fused ideals of fraternity and solidarity with norms of ethics and behavior."[42]

Yet a kursistka was defined not by brains alone. From the deliberately modest clothes they wore to the "democratic" mannerisms they cultivated, kursistki sought to present themselves as conscientious, engaged members of society, eager to tackle and solve the social problems of the day. As Richard Stites observed in his pathbreaking study of the women's liberation movement, "The atmosphere of mild poverty and free and easy equality among the women doubtless helped to nourish dreams of social justice."[43] Fresh from the bourgeois milieu of her parents' home in Vil'na, Vygodskaia experienced with pride and wonder the mood of radicalism that "infused" the halls of the Bestuzhev Courses. Although she herself seems never to have been affiliated with any of the revolutionary student movements of the day, Anna associated with radicals during her years in the capital and sympathized with their objectives of reforming Russian society: "The desire of female students in those days to strive for pure knowledge, combined with their desire to do good for the common people . . . these were like rays of light penetrating the dark and dreariness of Russian life."

Vygodskaia aptly describes the Bestuzhev Courses as "the one true liberal oasis in those reactionary times." The emperor Alexander

III had succeeded to the throne in 1881 following the assassination of his father, the tsar-emancipator Alexander II, and as Vygodskaia recalls, a "somber mood . . . had settled in." The new emperor was less inclined than his predecessor to countenance potential unrest and revolutionary discontent, and regarded universities and institutions of higher learning with suspicion. Women's higher education came under particular scrutiny. The regime's concerns were given voice by figures like the archconservative journalist Prince V. P. Meshcherskii, who described the women's courses in the capital as "a veritable sewer of anarchist disease."[44] Toward the end of her first year of study, Anna and her fellow kursistki were shocked to learn from a terse announcement in the government newspaper that the Bestuzhev Courses would be closed pending further notice. Historian Cynthia Whittaker notes that "only a tremendous outcry on the part of the general public" saved the Courses, which survived the announcement, albeit in curtailed and truncated form.[45] The Ministry of Education subjected the Bestuzhev Courses to an organizational overhaul that saw Nadezhda Stasova, the beloved director whom Vygodskaia described as "the heart and soul of our Courses," replaced by a more pliable administrator, caps set on the size of the incoming class, and quotas imposed on the number of "non-Christian" (Jewish) students admitted. By 1889–90, the year after Anna graduated, enrollment in the Courses stood at 144, down from 990 at the beginning of the decade. Applications to study at the Courses remained more or less constant through the 1890s and soared again in the early 1900s, but policy shifts obliged many Russian women to emigrate in search of the educational opportunities denied them at home.[46]

Life and Death

The radical revolutionary Vera Figner, a member of the Executive Committee of the People's Will, the conspiratorial circle that planned the assassination of Alexander II, recalled in her memoirs that her education at a fashionable girls' school in the 1860s had provided her with "a cultivated manner and a sense and need of comradeship" but had done her as much harm as good by fostering an "unnatural isolation from life and people."[47] It was this sense of detachment that Anna sought so fervently to overcome in her own education and upbringing. While some young women in the empire pursued higher education as a means to escape patriarchal control, achieve a sense of personal autonomy, secure economic independence, and perhaps find a suitable man for marriage, Vygodskaia, like many of her generation, describes her educational ambitions in idealistic terms: "I firmly believed that within these walls I could satisfy my thirst for knowledge, that scholarship would help me find the path toward independent, ideal, useful work, that I could live according to the dictates of my conscience."[48] Like many students on the eve of graduation, Anna experienced an existential crisis of sorts. She confided her fears to her mentor, Orest Miller, a celebrated literary scholar who taught at the Courses. Vygodskaia recalls Miller's sage advice: "It is possible to live according to one's conscience and be a useful person anywhere and under any conditions," he said. "One needs to rely on one's own instinct, and it will reveal the true path. Each person can do a great deal of good right where he is."

Anna's determination to become a "useful person" and work for the greater social good shaped the future course of her personal and professional development. She rejected the traditional feminine preserves of fashion and accessories, and she gently mocks her sister's fascination with such trifles as fancy dresses and tea towels for Anna's bridal trousseau. While the bourgeois Jewish women who summered at the resort community of Bel'mont, outside of Vil'na, gossiped about their fellow vacationers and promenaded in the latest fashions in their provincial setting, Vygodskaia sought authenticity—she tramped through the forest, went boating on the river, and embraced the natural world.

These descriptions of the quotidian are among the most revealing passages in the autobiography. In recalling her student days, Vygodskaia devotes much space to the rhythms and objects of everyday life—the romantic encounters and familial conflicts, the recreational activities and summer vacations—all of which made such a profound impression upon her. Vygodskaia arrived in St. Petersburg when rapid industrialization, urbanization, and mass consumerism enabled people of all social ranks and religious backgrounds—from the old landed elites, the nouveau riche, and high government officials to workers, middle-class professionals, and students—to shop in arcades and department stores and to take part in leisure-time activities such as theater and dance.[49] While she lived a "modest" life, working in the laboratory or listening to lectures in the first half of the day and studying or reading in the evenings, Anna also found the money (and the time) to listen to opera at the Mariinskii Theater and attend concerts by world-renowned pianists such as Anton Rubinstein and Józef Kazimierz Hofmann. On summer holidays, Anna spent her days enjoying recreational activities that were fashionable among youth of her social class: strolling in the countryside, boating, croquet, ring toss, swimming, and amateur theatrical productions.

During her student days in St. Petersburg, Anna confronted a world that challenged the ideals of propriety and modesty that had governed sexual conduct and behavior in the East European Jewish community. On several occasions Anna rejected the matches that her parents arranged for her in favor of advancing her education and asserting the freedom to choose her own groom on her own terms (until the second half of the nineteenth century, most Jewish girls were expected to marry by the age of sixteen, and boys by the age of eighteen). But even as she attempted to distance herself from the strict social codes that regulated sexuality and marriage in the Jewish community, including her parents' home, Anna refused to succumb to the temptations of city life. Although she recorded the transformation in sexual mores taking place around her ("In my day, female students would spend the night in male students' lodgings without thinking anything of it"), Anna observed that she herself was "quite naive and punctilious" in her private life. Eventually, after a lengthy courtship, Anna agreed to marry the medical student Mikhail Markovich Vygodskii (known by the initials M.M. in the autobiography), who was the son of a wealthy merchant-contractor and whom Anna describes as "nearer and dearer" to her than anyone else she had met in her life.[50] Anna was twenty-two years old at the time and had just finished her studies. She married Mikhail for emotional and intellectual reasons, without involving her parents in the decision. Such a match, considered progressive by the standards of the time, reflected many of the societal changes that helped transform the institution of marriage in the Jewish community as well as the criteria by which matches were made.[51]

It is at this point that Vygodskaia's memoir ends, and so does much of our knowledge of her professional and private experiences. According to Regina Weinreich's biographical sketch, not long after their wedding, Anna and Mikhail decided to move back to Bobruisk, where they cultivated a middle-class life for the next fifteen years. Mikhail practiced medicine, while Anna taught disadvantaged Jewish girls at a local Russian-language school.[52] After the Revolution of 1905, Anna and her husband relocated to Vil'na, and Anna worked in the newly opened private gymnasium founded by Sofia M. Gurevitch and Anna's former classmate at the Courses, P. P. Antokol'skaia. The school quickly acquired a reputation for its scholastic standards and progressive teaching methods. At the Gurevitch Gymnasium, the language of instruction was Russian, and children were taught mathematics, physics, natural sciences, art, Jewish history, religion, foreign languages, Russian literature, and Hebrew, at the request of parents. Although the gymnasium encountered numerous economic problems, it was nevertheless able to employ seven teachers, graduate over three hundred students between 1906 and 1917, and earn high praise from the local Jewish community.[53] Anna worked at the Gurevitch Gymnasium until around 1908, at which time she resigned her position, following the unexpected death of her husband. The loss of Mikhail dealt a severe emotional blow to Anna. She spent the next years of her life traveling to England, America, and Italy and acquainting herself with the pedagogical methods of the educator Maria Montessori. At the turn of the twentieth century, the Montessori system of education, organized around the basic principle that children should be given the freedom to guide their inner development, had become highly influential among reform-minded educators. Anna was part of an elite group of women, from all around the world, who undertook the work of establishing privately funded schools guided by the Montessori teaching method.[54]

With the eruption of the Great War, Vygodskaia decided to move from Vil'na to the safety of Moscow. The Russian Revolution of 1917 afforded Anna and other educators the opportunity to put their pedagogical theories into practice. In May 1918, Iuliia Ivanovna Fausek opened the first Montessori school in Petrograd; that same year, Vygodskaia founded the first Montessori school in Moscow.[55] Vygodskaia and her fellow reformers aimed at nothing less than the total reconfiguration of children's education, arguing that a new revolutionary society required an educational system organized on revolutionary lines, as well. In a 1920 pamphlet addressed to the mothers of young children, Vygodskaia reminded her readers that the political and social transformations in Russia afforded "freedoms and possibilities for the construction of a new kind of vibrant school life. . . . We will no longer teach—we will educate (*vospityvat'*)."[56] For Vygodskaia and other devotees of the Montessori method, upbringing (*vospitanie*) extended beyond the traditional lesson plans of reading, writing, and arithmetic. Children under the age of eight should be enrolled in special kindergartens, where their natural inclinations and abilities could be nurtured and channeled in positive directions by trained and committed educators. Children's curiosity, wonder, and sense of play should be encouraged, not stifled, so that boys and girls might cultivate and develop their personalities from an early age. Child rearing, Vygodskaia maintained, was a collaborative enterprise: "The tasks of schools have changed and expanded so much that no single educator can manage it without the close cooperation and participation of parents. . . . Our concern, as adults, is to provide children the kind of supportive surroundings where they can act independently and, consequently, develop freely."[57]

Such aspirations were all but impossible to achieve amid the hunger, privation, and general breakdown of social infrastructure that marked the years of civil war following the Bolsheviks' coming to power.[58] Vygodskaia's remarks at a pedagogy conference sponsored by the People's Commissariat of Enlightenment (Narkompros) reflected, too, her mounting frustration and exasperation with the bureaucratic obstacles impeding educational reform. Reiterating her arguments for the importance of preprimary education, Vygodskaia called upon her fellow delegates to involve kindergarten teachers more closely in the drafting of new educational models. "For some time now, in the Commissariat, the Preschool Commission and the School Commission meet side by side, separated by a single corridor . . . and yet we kindergarten teachers, laying the foundations for a new unified school, have no sense of the very nature of the structure being built atop our foundations. And so the members of the School Commission, building the entire structure themselves, debating fiercely each matter of masonry, proceed without inquiring whatsoever about the foundation that will be the basis for our glorious new structure. Can this go unaddressed? Of course not! In practical terms, it will come to the point where we will have to fix up, patch up, and make repairs, on account of which the strength and beauty of our new edifice will suffer."[59] In 1923, frustrated by the demands of an increasingly authoritarian and unresponsive regime, Vygodskaia left Soviet Russia and returned to Vil'na, which was then under Polish rule.[60]

The multiethnic and multiconfessional city had changed much in Anna's absence. The restoration of Polish independence after World War I now offered Jews the freedom to run schools, communal organizations, and cultural institutions in Yiddish, Hebrew, and Polish. The result was an unprecedented expansion of national Jewish political expression and experimentation in cultural activity.[61] In the interwar period, amid growing political extremism, Vygodskaia helped establish a Yiddish-language Montessori school for boys and girls from middle-class families. Housed on Wiwulska Street, Vygodskaia's school belonged to a network of Jewish-sponsored educational institutions known as the Tsentraler Bildungs Komitet (the Central Educational Committee). The umbrella organization operated kindergartens, elementary and high schools, a teachers' seminary, a library that housed over twenty thousand volumes in Jewish and European languages, and various children's clubs and associations.[62] According to Rachel Margolis, who studied there in the late 1920s, Vygodskaia's school "was considered very advanced." "All the pupils at school," Margolis recalled, "had little shelves with a colored sticker of some kind—in my case one with red cherries on it. I found it fun to study unfamiliar Yiddish letters. Then they began to give out cards with words and corresponding pictures on them, bright and nice looking. We sang a lot and did calisthenics. For Hanukkah we put together a musical."[63] Outside of her involvement in Montessori education, Vygodskaia also took an active role in several philanthropic organizations that were established by feminist activists to provide young Jewish women productive employment.[64]

The first volume of Vygodskaia's memoirs was published in 1938, and Dubnow's comments in the foreword suggest that plans for a second volume were already under way when the Second World War began the following year. The Nazi occupation of Vil'na in the summer of 1941 brought the flowering of Jewish cultural and educational life to an end. In September 1941, after months of terror, persecution, and murder, the Nazis proceeded to herd the remaining forty-six thousand Jews in Vil'na—men, women, and children—into the ghetto.[65] Vygodskaia was among them. In his ghetto diaries, the Jewish librarian and scholar Herman Kruk recorded that "Mrs. Anna Pavlovna has decided to continue writing. But where can you write in the ghetto, since altogether she has here 1.80 meters of space, a corner where she can only sleep, and not even do that properly? . . . The woman roams the streets all day with nothing to do." When a reading room was opened in the ghetto, Kruk set aside a small space at one of the tables for Vygodskaia to resume her writing. He confided to his diary that this small gesture brought the old woman to tears: "Now she sits at her table and writes. The person revives and now feels as if she were born anew."[66]

Anna Pavlovna Vygodskaia, aged seventy-five, died in September 1943, when the Nazis liquidated the Vil'na Ghetto.[67] The writings that occupied her final years have not survived.

THE STORY OF A LIFE

Foreword

Simon Dubnow

While confirming A. P. Vygodskaia's reference to my role as "instigator" in the writing of this memoir, I consider it my duty to explain my actions. I have always thought that the right to record one's reminiscences belongs not to writers, politicians, and other public figures alone, but indeed to all educated people whose lives have witnessed something more than the ordinary passing succession of generations from fathers to sons, that this right belongs to all those who have lived through an epoch of cultural upheavals and intense struggle between the old and young generations. Russian Jewry lived through precisely this kind of epoch in the second half of the nineteenth century and at the beginning of the twentieth, when the Enlightenment movement, the assimilationist movement, and the nationalist movement followed each on the heels of the other and declared themselves against the decrepit order of Orthodox Judaism and social exclusivity. This epoch found its full expression in Jewish belles lettres and in a series of memoirs, but there were very few memoirs written by women, memoirs that might present us with a picture of the Jewish woman's progress from the old way of life to the new, from the traditional role of the girl or mother of the ghetto to the free and emancipated Jewish woman, the builder of a new kind of family. It seems to me that the memoir of A. P. Vygodskaia fills in these gaps to a considerable degree.

In this first volume of memoirs, the reader is presented with a young, middle-class Jewish girl from Belorussia and her journey from the towns of the former Kingdom of Poland, to the Lithuanian capital of Vil'na, to the imperial Russian capital of Petersburg. This journey led the author from a primitive children's *heder*, through Polish-Russian elementary school and an all-Russian gymnasium, to the Higher Women's Courses in Petersburg, where a new generation of Jewish women was formed. In the immediate style of a lively story, without any literary embellishments, the author does not so much illustrate the spiritual life of that generation, with all of its ideological struggles, as present a picture of everyday life and all of the minor details to which male memoirists usually pay no heed, but which are so very important for the history of our material culture and national traditions. Particularly interesting is the description of the life of female students in Petersburg at a time when institutions of higher education were citadels of liberalism in reactionary Tsarist Russia. In the second volume, the author intends to tell of her excursions across Western Europe and of her pedagogical activities in Russia and Poland.

From the Author

It always seemed to me that the right to compose one's memoirs belonged exclusively to people who were famous for something or other, or to those who stood high above the average. A chance meeting with Professor Dubnow provided me the opportunity to converse with him from time to time and reminisce about the "good old days." It also put into my head the idea that even the memoirs of a person whose life was in no way remarkable might also be of great interest.

When I told the professor of various episodes from my childhood, episodes that cast in clear relief some of the customs and mores of the time, the primitiveness and simplicity of the old way of life, he remarked: "You tell everything so vividly, your stories are so characteristic of those bygone days, why don't you write everything down?"

To tell the truth, this suggestion struck a chord within me. I had always harbored a certain envy of those who write. Of course, my memoirs would not be a genuine literary effort, but rather a true account, stripped of all embellishment, of the lives of those people who had been near to me in those bygone years, a true account of the environment in which I was brought up, came of age, and lived. My purpose simply is to narrate. And so now, in offering my memories to the public, I feel obliged to express my deep gratitude to S. M. Dubnow, who for three years provided me with the moral support and courage necessary to write, in these our troubled times, about the peaceful life of the past.

CHAPTER ONE

Childhood Years

(Belorussia and Poland, 1870–80)

I

The memories of my early childhood always fill me with sorrow, perhaps because my mother's beautiful face was clouded by sadness. As far back as I can recall, our family consisted of just the three of us: my mother, me, and my sister, who was a few years older than I.

I barely remember my father. He worked someplace far away in Siberia and did not live with us. The story of Father's life was a common one for Jews in those days. When he was eighteen, he was married off to my mother, a sixteen-year-old orphaned girl from a good family with a modest dowry. They had to start living on their own and earn some money, but the head of the household was unable to do much of anything, for Father, you see, had received his education in a *heder*.[1] Father had a bit of money, and so he went into trade. Business, however, was slow, and yet they needed to live. What little money there was swiftly ran out, and the dowry was exhausted. It seems that God did not bless Father with business savvy. In this respect, he resembled Grandfather, who had also failed in business and thereafter worked the rest of his life as a cashier in a small office for a modest wage.

The family council, which consisted of Father, Mother, and Grandfather, jointly decided to make use of their family connections. Mother had wealthy relatives, the Fridliands, in St. Petersburg, some 1,500 *versts* from Bobruisk, where we lived at that time.[2] My mother was born in the small town of Mezherits, which is not so easy to find on a map. She had not traveled much and she knew little of the world; for her, Bobruisk might as well have been the capital of Russia. And yet my young, fragile, naive mother piled into a *buda*, something like a primitive stagecoach, and set out on a long, adventuresome journey of several weeks. What determination, energy, and sacrifice!

Mother, you see, married for love, and however strange it may appear, the primary motivation for this journey was the boundless love she possessed for her husband. Mother's heart was simply shattered at the sight of Father's grief and helplessness. How long the journey lasted and what indignities Mother endured along the way, I do not know. I have no memories of this, but according to my sister's tales, the Fridlands were not only well-to-do, but also well regarded in the community. They owned gold mines in Siberia.[3]

And so one day, Mother returned home with wonderful news: Father had been given a job in the Siberian mines—on the opposite side of the world, at the opposite end of the empire! The preparations began for Father's departure. Amid the excitement we didn't even stop to think that Father would be gone for three whole years. Three years in such a faraway place! Three years without seeing each other! But there was no time for distress; on the contrary, Mother was radiant with happiness. She was extraordinarily busy: she sewed and knitted everything for Father herself and managed all the household work (cooking, washing, and taking care of the two little children). In those days, the chores were anything but easy. It seems to me that the separation from Father was extremely difficult for Mother.

At this time, I will allow myself a brief digression. In order to give my impressions of the world in which we were brought up, I need to tell about my father's papa—our grandfather, who lived in the town of Bobruisk, the very town where I spent my childhood years.

II

Our grandfather was a dandy and an aesthete, and so he remained throughout his life. His sons maintained that he had a large ego besides. From his meager wages Grandfather somehow had managed to save up enough money to purchase elegant and expensive pipes, one-of-a-kind pieces of various shapes and sizes. He owned pipes that were half a meter long, as well as short, thick ones made out of ivory. Grandfather also acquired fine, decorative boxes that held smoking tobacco and snuff. All the old folks in those days took snuff, and so they were obliged to use large, dark handkerchiefs that were seldom very clean. Yet Grandfather's handkerchiefs were always pristine and decorated with pretty patterns.

Of course, Grandfather did not purchase his collectibles in Bobruisk. He once had a chance to visit Berlin, perhaps in connection with his lumber business. Thereafter, he would order various goods from there by catalogue. In this manner, he managed to compile a terrific collection. Nowadays, all of these objects would be valuable items on display in a museum. Grandfather carefully secured his treasures in a *secrétaire* (an old chest with secret drawers). I remember how all of his pipes were arranged in strict order according to their length. I also remember Grandfather's vests made out of thick damask silk: white, cream, chocolate-colored, and black, with pretty little flowers. Certain vests were designated for holidays, others for Saturdays, and the rest for daily wear. Since Grandfather spent great amounts of money on himself, while the family lived poorly, his youngest son, Grigorii, harbored a grudge against Grandfather for his whole life.

It is astonishing to me that in those days there could be such an aesthete, such a lover of all things beautiful, in such an out-of-the-way place as Bobruisk, a town famous only for its swamps. This remains a mystery to me to this day. By nature Grandfather was a gentleman, a man of most honest principles, who never offended anyone, although, truth be told, he never did much good for anyone either. His love for beautiful things did not prevent him, however, from taking as his second wife a woman who was unrefined, shrewish, and, moreover, not entirely honest when it came to business matters. She used to make a mixture of different grades of tea and sell it at the bazaar on the sly. In this manner, she was able to scrape together a bit of money, thereby supplementing as well as she could the family's modest budget. As we children always said, it wasn't Grandfather who married her; it was she who married him.

I remember to this day how afraid I was of this old woman, with her hawklike nose and her Baba Yaga eyes. Especially frightening was the enormous headgear she wore atop her shaved, bare head.[4] This contraption consisted of a black satin cap that covered her entire head. Underneath the cap she wore a wig with two long, cylindrical rolls of hair that narrowed at the ends and lay perpendicular to the part in her wig. On top of the cap was a wreath of interlaced ribbons of all the colors of the rainbow. This wreath was decorated with sprigs of artificial flowers that clashed with the faded ribbons. The old woman wore this headgear throughout the entire two years that I knew her. She never took it off except at night.[5]

As she left in the morning for the market with her tea bags in hand, Grandmother would bark out instructions to the cook concerning lunch. The cook lived in a separate room with her husband, in exchange for which she cooked and cleaned our house. Before leaving for the market, the old woman would hurriedly dish out orders: "Make borscht with mushrooms! And mushroom soup, too!" This combination of dishes attests to her rich culinary imagination. When she returned home from the market (after Mother's death we lived for a period of time with Grandfather), I would hide in a corner so that I wouldn't have to see this old monster. On Sundays the old woman would raise an incredible fuss and would curse the cook for not having polished the bronze candlesticks (there were eight of them). You see, she would say, it'll soon be Sabbath again, and the candlesticks are still standing here since Friday evening prayers!

Grandfather couldn't stand his wife and never spoke with her. She would fly around the house like a witch, while Grandfather always walked with calm, measured steps. I remember how he used to wake up from his afternoon nap, take one of his many pipes from the secrétaire, and sit by the window in his redwood armchair. He usually wore an elegant yarmulke on his head, gold eyeglasses, and a patterned silk robe that was tied around the waist by a thick cord. Grandfather's beard was gray and rounded. He was even able to skillfully gnaw on the ends and, in this fashion, give it proper shape: to cut one's beard with scissors was considered a great sin in those days. Grandfather would sit by the window like a sultan, holding a long pipe in his incredibly beautiful hands! He would be served his tea, strong as beer, in a large etched glass in a silver cup holder. Grandfather would look out the window as he sipped his tea. Passersby would admire his handsome features and greet the old man. This made him happy.

Our grandfather was not very talkative. I remember when he once came to visit us in Vil'na. This happened many years later, when we were living there with our father and stepmother. Father went to greet Grandfather at the station, which was about a six- or seven-minute walk from our home. Stepmother greeted our guest at the door. The gloomy, taciturn looks on the faces of father and son troubled her, and she asked in a frightened voice: "Faitel', what happened? Something bad?" Father calmly replied: "Nothing happened. It's just that halfway home we ran out of things to talk about."

Enough said of Grandfather and his wife for now. I will have to return to him later, when I describe our life after Mother's death.

III

When I ask myself where I get the things that I write about, it seems to me that all of this has been lurking below the surface, in the realm of the subconscious, for many years. Now all the images and events appear before me as though alive, and when woven together, they form a picture of the past.

I will now tell about our life with Mother. By the standards of the day, our apartment was, as they say, a *bombonerka*—small, but cozy. I remember the times when Mother would be away and her nosy girlfriends would peek in our window, admiring the cleanliness and neatness of the decor. However, there was nothing special about our apartment. All the homes in our town were poor and neglected, with tiny windows, uneven floors, and low ceilings. I especially remember the enormous stove in the kitchen. We did not have fashionable furniture, as our grandfather did: we had simple tables, chairs, beds, and a dresser. But what made our apartment distinctive? What, besides the cleanliness, made it attractive? All the tables in the so-called living room were covered with woolen tablecloths made from fringed doilies sewn together with wool. On the oval table there stood a lamp atop a special stand. This stand was actually a circular piece of cardboard wrapped in colored, patterned paper and surrounded by artificial grass made out of thick yarn threads of different shades of green. Arranged amid the grass were artificial flowers fashioned out of thin, spiraled wire. You could take a little piece of wire, bend it in the shape of a leaf, and wrap it in wool. Five of these little leaves joined together formed a single flower. Primitive, but such was life in those days! From the glass lampshade hung a small canopy, a piece of silk richly embroidered with different-colored beads, very much in fashion at the time. Similar canopies hung above the silver candlesticks, which stood on two small tables. Mother would pray before these candlesticks on Fridays. One pair of them remains with us to this very day.

All of these decorations were made by Mother's own hands. But there was more. On the walls were small pieces of embroidered handiwork, framed and under glass. There was a miniature cross-stitched landscape done in wool on white canvas, depicting people, trees, houses, and so forth. The work was extraordinarily detailed and laborious. Decoratively stitched curtains hung on the windows— once again, Mother's handiwork. Many years later, while I was in London in 1912, studying at the Teachers Institute, I was assigned to embroider a pattern. I closed my eyes and called to mind those motions that Mother used to make, and thanks to this I was able to grasp the subtleties of embroidery faster than the others in my class. This fact should be of interest to a psychologist.

I still get teary-eared when I recall how our mother, beautiful in body and soul, with her large, pensive eyes, would bend over her sewing frames and sing sorrowful songs while she stitched. I remember one song in particular: "And perhaps my dreams are senseless, senseless tears and heartache." This song always ended with uncontrollable weeping; Mother would stop her work, dash into her room, and lock the door. She was a very proud woman and carefully hid her anguish from both her family and outsiders. Some time later she would reemerge calm and collected, gently stroke our heads, and resume her daily work.

Mother was an excellent housekeeper—not only did she wash the clothes, but she ironed them with an expert hand. She sewed all our undergarments and dresses, both for us and for herself. I especially remember the holiday dresses she made for us to wear at the wedding of one of our relatives. They were made out of muslin, with trimmings, and decorated with flowers. Mother could not go to the wedding: she lay in bed with unnaturally swollen cheeks and feverish eyes. By this time she was sick with raging tuberculosis, from which she died soon thereafter. I remember how she still straightened our dresses while she lay in bed, admiring us, her eyes shining with pride. She asked us to bring her a pinch of salt in a tiny bag: with her own hands she sewed them to the hem of our skirts, so that, God forbid, we would not be given the evil eye at the wedding!

A mother is the source of light for each of us throughout our entire lives. Rest in peace, our blessed, dear mother.

IV

I can only imagine the emotional suffering, not to mention the physical ones, that our poor mother endured during her illness, conscious of the hopelessness of her situation and the impossibility of seeing her husband before she died, while suffering with the thought that her little orphans would be left without anyone to watch over them! Despite her love toward us, Mother raised us strictly. We always looked neat, tidily dressed and nicely combed. I remember when I was five years old, with flaxen hair braided into two ponytails, tied together with a narrow piece of striped calico. My bluish gray, sparkling eyes apprehended much and looked at everything in wonder. I was a plain child, and I think that it was in vain that Mother took such pride in me and was so fearful of the jealous glances of others. But such is love!

My sister, three years older than I, was my exact opposite: pretty, lively, spirited, and temperamental. She smiled good-naturedly at everyone, had an exceptionally kind heart, and was unselfish even as a young child.

One episode readily comes to mind from our childhood that confirms this description. While we were still living with Mother, Grandfather was raising his youngest daughter from the first marriage (he had no children from his second wife). This daughter, Polia, was only three years older than my sister, but she was already extraordinarily mature, having mastered the entire Bible. Aunt Polia was self-taught, with an astonishing memory, and a critical outlook on life far beyond her years. She was not very talkative, but extremely observant and picked up on anything humorous—in short, a little grown-up. She seldom paid any attention to my sister. My sister and aunt represented two extreme personality types: one sanguine, the other choleric. Once, it so happened, while our mother was out, Polia graced us with a visit. My sister was overjoyed. I remember how Aunt Polia sat so pompously at the table in profound silence while my sister wore herself out trying to engage her in conversation. Although I was there the entire time, no one paid any attention to me. All of a sudden, my sister realized that our visitor must be hungry. Polia declined everything that was offered to her, but in the end magnanimously declared that she could eat a little cold sorrel soup. My sister—clever, quick, and talented, just like Mother—ran to the kitchen and began to prepare dinner for the three of us. The bread was cut, the butter spread, the cucumbers peeled, and, the most important thing, the soup was ready to go. But alas, there was no sour cream to mix into the soup! My poor sister tore the kitchen apart, searching everywhere, but could not find any. Suddenly, it dawned upon her that she could use milk instead of sour cream. And so she poured in a generous dollop of milk, since she was making the soup especially for Aunt Polia, who was ever so picky about her food. Triumphantly, my sister brought the cold sorrel soup with cucumbers and hard-boiled eggs and, of course, gave the first bowl to Aunt. Our aunt took the spoon and brought it to her lips. She very coolly put the spoon back and muttered through her teeth: "Sorrel soup with milk!"

Needless to say, our aunt did not take another spoonful. My sister was on the brink of tears and assured Polia that she had poured in only the tiniest portion of milk. Nothing she said, however, could help matters any. Out of politeness, Aunt Polia stayed for a little while longer and then went home, greatly offended. We'd lost our appetites, and so we sat there sadly, waiting for Mother to come home.

V

Despite worries and troubles of the household, and her constant longing for her husband, Mother found time to educate herself. Uncle Grigorii, father's youngest brother, first pushed her in this direction. He was her first teacher and enlightener, to use the terminology of the times, and it was he who introduced her to Russian literature.

Uncle Grigorii also took an active role in our education. I can't say that my sister and I were delighted with his pedagogical methods—he would make us stand in a corner for a long time, sometimes even with our hands raised high above our heads. How long we stood depended on the severity of the infraction. After a period of time, however, we were allowed to walk up to our mother, kiss her hand, and ask for forgiveness. As soon as my sister ran off to Mother, I would follow her. But what were we supposed to do when we were required to stand in separate rooms? I remember how horrible I felt when I once found out that my sister had been off running and playing for a long time already, while I had stood and served out my whole sentence! We were never beaten, however, except on only one occasion, which I will later recount because it produced such a strong effect on my impressionable nature and has without question left a mark on my psyche.

Before Uncle Grigorii got involved in our education, we attended a heder for girls for a brief time. But I had barely learned the alphabet, which was no small feat in those days. I remember only one episode from those days. Once I was walking home from heder and it began to rain, and without thinking I pulled my dress over my head and ran down the middle of the street (we had no sidewalks in those days), singing loudly my mother's favorite song: "And perhaps my dreams are senseless, senseless tears and heartache." We spoke Yiddish in those days, and so I did not understand a single word of the song. I had a good voice, by the way, and I sang in perfect pitch.

Uncle Grigorii didn't stay in Bobruisk for very long. He wanted to enroll in the Teachers Institute and in the end left for Vil'na.[6] It was then that the tensions began between him and his egotistical father. Uncle Grigorii did not have much money for his studies. I think Mother managed to help him from the pittance that Father sent home.

Although Mother's formal studies stopped after Uncle Grigorii left, her thirst for knowledge only multiplied tenfold. I remember Mother paid a tutor to come and teach her arithmetic and other subjects. In those days, this type of behavior was unheard of for a married woman with a family, especially one who was separated from her husband. In our town, such a thing was simply not done. But Mother paid no attention to gossip, and she always tried to stay away from gossipy women. I can only imagine how those women ran their mouths! Mother, incidentally, did not say a word to anyone about her studies, and so we children instinctively felt that we should keep quiet as well.

How did we pass the time in our early childhood? We lived a free and easy life and spent a great portion of the day in games with our playmates. The only thing that Mother required of us was that we return home for lunch and dinner in a timely fashion and not stain or tear our dresses. After having fed us she would clean us up, and we would once again go out and play.

I remember that one day our games nearly ended in tragedy. We were playing hide-and-seek in a large courtyard, where piles of wood were stacked. In the courtyard there stood a big barn stuffed half full with hay and all sorts of rubbish, including some old trunks with rusty hinges. We each hid in different parts of the courtyard. I hid in the barn and suddenly thought of a brilliant place to hide: I opened one of the trunks with the rusty hinges, climbed in ever so carefully, curled up, and closed the lid. My prediction came true: no one found me. But lying for a long time in an almost completely sealed box, I began to feel as if I couldn't breathe, and I screamed out in a voice that sounded nothing like my own. Fortunately, a workman passing by heard my cries, opened the trunk, and saved the tiny, foolish heroine. My playmates were so engrossed in their game that they had not even noticed I was gone.

On another occasion a misfortune befell my sister. Early one morning after breakfast, we left, as usual, neatly dressed and combed, to go play in the courtyard. Beside our porch there stood a barrel with water; not every courtyard had its own well, and so the water carrier brought the pails to the kitchen. When my sister saw the water barrel, she suddenly exclaimed: "I'll pull out the stopper and plug it right back in again!" No sooner said than done. She took it out all right, but she couldn't put it back in again and was soon drenched with water, from head to toe, as though she'd just stepped out of Niagara Falls. All of the water flowed out of the barrel. My sister was frightened, so she ran away to hide somewhere and wait until her dress dried. That meant she did not make it home in time for lunch, and so the poor soul had to serve out the customary punishment—standing in the corner! Mother faithfully put Uncle Grigorii's maxims into practice when it came to raising the children.

VI

The life of a small town flows along peacefully, monotonously for years, like a tiny stream through a valley. But no matter how small the stream, its waters are always in motion, sometimes even roiling into a mighty river. Not so with a provincial town: it is eternally immersed in lethargy and quietly muddles along in its own swamp. The people there toil and live grimly, monotonously, inertly, just like their fathers and grandfathers before them, without any expectation of change.

But in those days, one could meet young people who wanted to pull themselves up out of the provincial mud. Both of my uncles, Grigorii and Avraam Paperna, were such pioneers.[7] But they were exceptions. The folks who ran these small towns were conservative Jews. And doesn't everyone know that it is their aim to keep life locked in a standstill? Bobruisk thought of itself as an island surrounded by impassable swamps. People here sealed themselves off from the rest of the world. New ideas, the new trends of the 1870s, barely penetrated this place. Those few individuals who were touched by these ideas could not bear the spiritual impoverishment of their surroundings. They sought to break free from this stagnant swamp, and once having broken free, they would never again return. This is why we cannot speak of any type of cultural progress or the birth of an intelligentsia in Bobruisk in those days.

But with the building of the railroad, which coincided with our first departure from Bobruisk, new intellectual currents began to reach us.[8] I can't say, though, that these ideas produced any noticeable effect on the mind-set of our town. In those days, any kind of reform was greeted with opposition and caught on extraordinarily slowly. Half a century would pass before one could discern any development or growth in towns such as Bobruisk. I do not exaggerate: some forty years passed from the day I was born till the second time I left Bobruisk, and I can't say that our town had changed noticeably throughout this entire time. Only in 1906, during the period of the so-called political spring, did our town finally breathe new life.[9]

I've painted a picture of what daily life was like in our dead little town, so it's not at all surprising, then, that Father's arrival—a private, purely family affair—created such a stir throughout all of Bobruisk. A few months before Father's arrival, Mother came back to life. Her entire appearance was transformed. She walked with a spring in her step, her anxiety vanished, her pensive eyes shone with happiness, and she no longer sang her melancholy songs. The household chores increased twofold, perhaps even threefold: we whitewashed the walls, fixed up the house, darned wool, and sewed, all without taking a break. It was as if Mother tried to use work as a way to make the waiting go by faster. We children were swept up as well, not in the work itself, but in the mood of joyous anticipation. In all honesty, though, I had not even the faintest recollection of my father. Our nervous anticipation mounted because we did not know when exactly this special moment would occur. It seemed to me that I kept hearing from every corner: "Father is coming, Father is coming!" Even in my sleep I heard these words. And though Mother appeared as calm and collected as ever, we sensed her inner excitement, and we were happy for her. She even started chatting with the gossipy neighbors; they visited us quite frequently now, and Mother would smile and talk with them. With such a heavy workload, she paid less attention to how neatly we were dressed, and we were quite happy about this—at times, we would play from morning to night. Everything in the house sparkled; no one was allowed in the living room, lest, God forbid, a speck of dust might blow in. Everything and everyone was ready, and the house was in tip-top shape.

As the wait dragged on, Mother would feel sad and sometimes even cry. We knew better than to disturb her. But what could we possibly understand? We wouldn't go off to play as much as we used to; we would stay closer to home. Often we would run out to the highway that led into town and stand there for long periods of time, staring first to one side and then the other, and then run home to bring the sad news—"We didn't see him!" With every thump of a passing wagon, my sister and I would leap out into the street—is it Father? Without being told, we took upon ourselves the task of watching and listening for Father. Although our mother appeared calm, she was quite nervous on the inside and did not leave the house.

Finally, the joyous day arrived. We were not the only ones filled with anticipation; so was the entire town. From afar, we could already spot the enormous buda, stirring up great clouds of dust. People ran out from every porch; everyone looked on, felt happy for us, and rejoiced: "Here comes Faitel' Paperna!"

My sister and I were quite emotional. To think of all that we had gone through with Mother as we awaited Father's return! We didn't dash out to hop on board the buda and hug and kiss our guest. Instead, we rushed home so that we would be the first to break the joyous news: "He's here!" When the buda stopped in front of our house, a whole crowd of curious onlookers gathered around it. Mother held back her emotions, apparently because she did not want her first encounter with Father to take place in front of so many strangers. Not only did she not walk out to the porch, but she even withdrew to her room and awaited our guest with trepidation.

Father stepped out of the carriage and anxiously began to look around, searching for her with his eyes. He gave us a quick kiss, without smiling. We kissed him back, and he asked us with alarm: "Where's Mama? Where is she?"

From that moment forth, it was a real celebration at our house. Father was the center of our attention, and Mother happily bustled about. Although we were children, the sight of Mother's joyous face—our mother, whom we loved so much—calmed us. I don't know what would have happened if Father had remained with us for good; in all probability, I would have grown jealous of the attention Mother paid him. Yet his stay in our household did not last long. Shortly after Father's arrival, I suffered a great indignity for which he was to blame. This shame weighed on my soul for the duration of his stay, and I have remembered it throughout my entire life.

Even to this day I've been regarded, and not without reason, as someone who is easily offended. Who knows? Perhaps the indignity that Father inflicted upon me determined the highly sensitive way in which I interact with people, something that has remained with me for the duration of my life. So what happened? It seems an insignificant event, one that would have passed unnoticed by less delicate and impressionable children, but for me it was a tremendous blow. A few days after his arrival, Father—whom Mother adored so much, who seemed to us the center of our existence, and whom we put on a pedestal—flogged me with birch branches, without any warning and without any prior admonitions!

My crime consisted of the following: we children were playing by the porch, and we probably got carried away. I didn't have time to remove myself to a private place before the call of nature took over, and so I relieved myself right there and then on the porch. After the punishment, I no longer wanted to be in Father's presence, and for the rest of my life, I remained on rather cool terms with him. Now I think that he punished me only to show off his paternal authority.

I have no more recollections of Father's stay in our house. I don't even remember his departure.

VII

It was from my sister that I learned how Mother's illness began. The infection in her lungs spread with catastrophic speed. After Father left, Mother gave birth to her third daughter. Apparently, though, pregnancy and childbirth expedited the illness to which she was already predisposed. This plus melancholy, loneliness, and the strenuous conditions of her life helped to aggravate further the infection in her lungs.

One can judge the severity of the illness by the fact that, despite our tight financial situation and notwithstanding the separation from her children, Mother went to Samara to take the *koumiss* cure, leaving us in the care of our eldest aunt.[10] Mother returned in better health, but a heavy blow awaited her at home: her beloved, our little baby girl, just eighteen months old, was no longer among the living.

There are people who are able to cope with grief. Ordinarily, as time passes, the feeling of self-preservation takes hold, the pain gradually subsides, and people return to their customary ways of life. This is not what happened to Mother. She not only grieved for the little one but suffered terribly as well; she reproached herself for leaving us for two whole months in the care of our relatives. As soon as Mother came back, she began to wither and melt, just like a wax candle. The fatal blow came when she caught a cold. It seems that she came down with the cold in the synagogue, which she regularly attended on Sabbath.

I remember that she had but one formal dress, which she wore only on Saturdays and holidays—it was silk, stiffened with crinoline, wrapped tightly around her waist, and girded with a narrow, silver sash that looked a bit like what they wear in the Caucasus. The skirt was wide and separated into gathers. Over the dress Mother wore a short velvet cape with fringes, and on her head a pretty wig with curls that dropped down to her neck, decorated with a narrow velvet ribbon. On holidays she also wore jewelry: a malachite brooch in a gold setting; long malachite earrings; a gold necklace with a locket; a gold, handmade bracelet, trimmed with blue enamel that could be adjusted to fit snugly around the wrist. The brooch and the bracelet are still with me to this day—these are the relics I have of Mother. She was quite lovely and everyone admired her. The gossipy neighbors said that Mother had the evil eye put on her in the synagogue.

Mother took to her bed and never got up again. I remember the silent, suffering gaze that she fixed on us when we walked into her room. As the illness progressed we were allowed to see her less frequently. And as the days passed, the more she suffered—I was frightened to even look at her. How much willpower it must have taken for her to refrain from kissing us even once! Her eyes grew larger and more feverish, her cheeks more flushed. Despite all her efforts, she could no longer even manage a smile for us. Everyone could see how Mother was suffering, and we were no longer permitted to go in and see her. Sensing that the end was near, our relatives brought her to Grandfather's house.

After that we never saw her alive again, though we were brought to see her one final time. Mother's body rested on some straw on the floor of the living room, covered with a coarse, black cloth, decorated in the handmade embroidery into which she had poured so much of her love, soul, and tears! When we paid our final respects to Mother, our aunt carried me in her arms. And what did I see? Our loving, beautiful mother, our guardian angel thrown down on a pile of straw and covered in a terrible black cloth! Not even her pretty face could be seen. I became frightened: I began to shake and shout out loud, grabbing my aunt's neck and hiding my face so as not to look upon this horror. They took me away, of course. And then we were once again brought to Grandfather's house. In all probability, the funeral took place that same day. Neither her husband whom she loved so much nor her children were there to attend the funeral. She was twenty-six years old.

VIII

The transition from our home, where there was so much love, poetry, and beauty, to the atmosphere of Grandfather's house depressed me. Our young, loving, pretty mother had been replaced by an ugly, mean, old woman! Grandfather kept silent and did not involve himself with household matters; he dutifully put in his time at work and worried only about himself. Our aunts paid little attention to us—they lived their own solitary lives, trying to have as little as possible to do with their old stepmother, our grandmother, whom no one loved. During the time we stayed with Grandfather, I don't remember playing with other children in as carefree a fashion as I had before.

You don't skip verses when you're singing a song. And so, in describing this period of my life, I can't keep silent about one of my sins. It happened like this: Mother was buried, if I am not mistaken, on a Friday. And the next morning I was already out playing with other children, hopping about on one leg. Grandfather lived on the highway (this was the only paved road in our town). Since it was a holiday, the men left for the synagogue in the morning, and the women, who were half-dressed but already washed and combed, sat on the bench on the porch, chitchatting amiably among themselves. I especially remember two of our neighbor women; gossipmongers called them the two old maids, though they were probably all of twenty-one or twenty-two years old. That morning, they were wearing starched petticoats with pleated frills and loose, comfortable blouses of the same material and with the same frills. They sat opposite our house, and we children were playing in the middle of the road. Suddenly, I looked across the street at our neighbors, and they looked back at me. They shook their heads back and forth and whispered something to one another. As I noticed their glance, it hit me like a thunderbolt. I suddenly remembered our great sorrow; I remembered that Mother was no longer alive. I started sobbing hysterically, and I wanted to run home. But we no longer had a home to call our own. There was no one to lean on. I no longer had Mother's warm breast on which I could cry to my heart's content.

***

Grandfather's house consisted of four rooms and a kitchen. The entrance was through the kitchen. To the right was a relatively large room where we slept—Aunt Polia in one bed, and my sister and I in the other. A large dining table stood by the window. To the left of the kitchen was a small room, where the old cook lived with her husband, who left for work early in the morning, day in, day out, and returned home in the evening. Across from the kitchen was the so-called living room, with its fashionable redwood furniture. This was where we ate our meals on Saturdays and holidays. Against the wall between the windows there was an enormous sofa, with overstuffed cushions and a tall, wooden back. Nearby stood an oval-shaped coffee table and, across from it, Grandfather's chest of drawers, or secrétaire, as it is fashionable to say nowadays. Grandfather had an entire chain of keys for this secrétaire. There was also a second, smaller cabinet with glass doors. Inside were stored candlesticks of various sizes and silver boxes, or *pushkes*,[11] as they were called in Yiddish; one of these pushkes—an oval one—was set aside specifically for *esrog*.[12] Also behind the glass were various holiday dishes: a silver wine cup with which grandfather said the *havdala*[13] on Saturday evenings, smaller wine cups used especially for the seder,[14] and a silver tray that was half the size of the large table, used solely when guests came over on holidays. There was also a tiny fish made of silver that grandfather lifted up to his nose after some special sort of prayer,[15] thick, blue, cut-glass carafes of various sizes that were used for vodka and wine, as well as matching shot glasses and glass dishes of various sizes.

Our oldest aunt, Grunia, slept on the big sofa between the windows. After supper, Grandfather would stretch out on the sofa and relax. Usually so silent and calm, Grandfather was quite noisy while he slept: he puffed, whistled, moaned, and snored so loudly that not only the walls but the whole house shook! The old folks' bedroom was situated to the right of the living room. Two simple wooden beds stood there, with an entire mountain of pillows of various sizes that looked like the Eiffel Tower, as well as a chest of drawers and a large linen cabinet with two deep drawers on the bottom. The floors were washed once a week and always sprinkled with yellow sand—to keep things tidy, and perhaps for decoration.

IX

We lived with Grandfather for about a year. Left to the whims of fate, my sister and I roamed around this uncomfortable home without any supervision whatsoever. My recollections from this period are fragmentary pictures, unconnected scenes, but so vivid that they have been preserved in my memory. I remember, for example, our Saturday meals. Grandfather would come home from the synagogue dressed handsomely and with great care. As I mentioned before, we would eat at the table in the living room. There were so many hors d'oeuvres: plain herring, on top of which Grandfather himself would pour the finest olive oil (I remember the handsome motions of his hands), chopped herring, chopped liver, radishes cut in thin slices and served with onions and goose fat, calves' feet (*petcha*), and cold stuffed fish with a healthy dose of black pepper. After these, came a whole series of dishes that made up the *cholent*: bouillon with kasha made from beans and pearl barley, *tzimmes* made from prunes and potatoes that were cooked overnight on a large stove.[16] For dessert, we had kugel made from flour and finely minced goose fat, with some sort of spices for taste.[17] In short, the meals were plentiful and rich. It seems that back then our stomachs could fit more food than they do today.

When Grandfather came home from the synagogue, he would usually sit in his chair by the window, where his favorite cat rested. It was interesting to watch the cat sit there for hours, peacefully and so well mannered, as he awaited Grandfather's arrival. He would never stoop to thievery: he wouldn't even sniff or lick at a morsel of food! The cat knew full well that Grandfather would take care of him after he'd fed himself, and so he patiently waited his turn. This always amused me.

We did not have much in common with the old lady. Our grandmother did not have a very kind, loving heart, and she did not worry too much about us orphans. Ordinarily, after returning home from the bazaar, she would slip on a cotton apron over her loose caftan and fasten it in the back with a bow. Once she had bellowed out a bunch of terse and noisy orders to the cook, she would head off to the bedroom, open one of the dresser's wide bottom drawers, and pour a handful of nuts into her apron. With this supply of nuts she would sprawl out on the sofa, her legs spread wide. This position was not especially elegant, but apparently quite comfortable.

With a serious and businesslike demeanor, she would go to work: with the right side of her jaw she would crack the nuts and stuff the shelled pieces in her left cheek, performing this task with exceptional speed and dexterity. In fact, she looked just like a nutcracker. I watched her with curiosity and with a sliver of hope that perhaps a few of the nuts might fall to the floor. And indeed, sometimes, after having eaten her fill, she would pick out some of the very smallest nuts from what was left over and give them to us. After stuffing her gut, she would sit there on the sofa in a funny pose without moving for a long period of time, so that she could calmly digest all that she had just consumed. Aunt Polia would manage to replicate this pose quite successfully many years later. As she sat with her legs spread out, Grandmother would pull both ends of her apron tight so that the shells would not fall out; her right elbow would lean up against her left palm, and the right hand would prop up her chin; her mouth was closed and drawn sharply downward toward the left cheek. If I were a sculptor, I would have molded this figure. It would have been worth it to preserve for posterity the old woman's face, with her sharp features, spiteful expression, and a look of sheer determination!

* * *

During the time we lived with Grandfather, construction began on the railroad. I remember how enormous crowds gathered on the highway one Saturday to watch the first wagon pass by on the rails. Soon we too would make use of this means of transport. Father was still in Siberia, and at his request Grandfather took us to be educated with Uncle Grigorii, who had been such a good friend to my late mother. At that time, he lived in Zakrochim, a small Polish town not far from Plotsk, and directed the elementary school there; he was married to a woman who was from Plotsk. On the road to Zakrochim, Grandfather taught us to count in Polish. We repeated after him the foreign words, but by the time we arrived, we had managed to learn to count only to five, because we just could not remember the Polish word for five—*pięć*. But perhaps we had a bad teacher—what kind of Polish could Grandfather have known?

X

We left Bobruisk by rail, but then we had to travel many more miles in a buda. We received a joyous and heartfelt welcome in Zakrochim. Even our aunt, who was meeting us for the first time, greeted us very warmly. Zakrochim was far smaller than Bobruisk, but it looked nicer. I didn't see any mud puddles, which still dotted Bobruisk even twenty years later when I returned. Nor do I recall, for example, pigs bathing in mud on the streets of Zakrochim, as they did back in my hometown. Some streets were even paved, and stone houses could be found in the town. The population here was entirely Polish. The Russian language was almost never heard, and there were few Jews as well.[18] Life was modest, peaceful, almost idyllic, and everyone kept to himself.

Uncle Grigorii held the post of senior teacher in the Zakrochim elementary school. He received a very modest wage—probably not much more than the twenty-five rubles that Father paid for our tuition and room and board. A Polish baker owned the building that housed the school. It was a two-story building; we had never seen such structures in Bobruisk. The owner and his large family lived on one half of the ground floor. The bakery was here as well. The school occupied the other half of the floor, with two big rooms, one for the older students and the other for the younger ones. Uncle's assistant taught the younger students.

Our apartment was on the floor above. You entered through the dark kitchen, enormous and almost empty. The next room was small and narrow, with two windows and a cupboard for dishes and food. There was a simple table pushed up against the wall between the windows, and a small iron bed, which stood—none too steadily—on crooked legs. This was the bed my sister and I shared. The room next door, which had a balcony, was Aunt and Uncle's bedroom. Their daughter, who was born during our stay, slept here as well. Later she became a fiery Social Democrat, who spent a great part of her youth in prison. There was also a third room, but it stood empty, because there was not enough furniture to go around.

***

Our aunt was a simple, plain woman, uneducated but possessed of a kindly soul. She loved everyone, sympathized with everyone, and wished everyone well. She was a hard worker, tall and ungainly, with big, chapped hands covered with calluses because she was constantly washing the linen (imagine—for five people!) or whipping something up on the stove.

Our table was a very simple one. Most days for supper we had soup with a small piece of meat. Sometimes instead of a meat soup, there would be a fish soup with potato dumplings. This is a Polish national dish, prepared in the following manner: you mix flour, water, and raw grated potatoes into a firm dough, and then separate the dough by hand into long strips. These are then thrown into salted boiling water, with a few tiny fish tossing about (more for show than anything else). A great big dose of pepper and onion is poured in for some spice. An inexpensive delight!

The dumplings, however, were hard as rocks; you had to swallow them practically whole, without chewing them. I was always a fussy eater, but I remember that our aunt ate them with a hearty appetite. Although she had done the work of three, she wouldn't eat a bite from morning till afternoon, by which time we had already had two meals! Uncle Grigorii didn't eat the same meals we did. Our aunt would cook something special for him because he was in poor health and suffered from weak lungs. The military doctor who treated him had long warned that teaching would be the death of him. But what could be done, how was one supposed to live? I remember how he would come upstairs at noon during his break (lessons lasted from morning till noon and from two o'clock to four o'clock). He would stop and lean against the wall and start coughing, hacking up phlegm into a glass, which was soon filled. He would be covered in a cold sweat, and then, exhausted, he would go lie down and rest, only to be called out for supper. Aunt prepared hearty bouillon and a big beefsteak for Uncle every day. She was a master in the kitchen—the beefsteak came out wonderfully, and the meat retained all its juices. As we swallowed down our plain dumplings, we would rejoice if Uncle liked his beefsteak and ate every bite. Aunt's face would light up at this: "Eat up for your health, dear Grigurele" (that's what she called him).

Our Uncle Grigorii was an exceptional man: despite a humble education, he distinguished himself by the great breadth of his intellect. How interested he was in everything, and how he grasped and took in all the newest intellectual trends of the day! He was a liberal in the best sense of the word. He read a great deal and was interested in contemporary literature and especially in politics; his paper of choice was always the liberal *Golos* (The Voice).[19] He spent his free hours in long, private conversations with others of a liberal mind-set. Uncle Grigorii was a man of strong character. At that time, only those types of people could move up in the world: back then, not everyone learned to read and write in childhood, since education was not mandatory, as it is today. Individuals like my uncle strived for knowledge, for enlightenment, for the development of that which, for them, was truly an organic necessity. A person who strived for education had to possess great persistence and endurance, and had to be prepared for all sorts of sacrifices, including many years of privation, in order to achieve one's goals—the acquisition of knowledge to work for the good of the people, the *narod*. "Man lives not by bread alone!"—such was the slogan of the best people in those days.

Teaching paid poorly compared to other professions, but in the educated person's mind, teachers stood on a higher plane than all other representatives of the intelligentsia. Almost every teacher was a true bearer of enlightenment.

XI

Uncle Grigorii was well respected in the town. He carried out his duties conscientiously and with great ability. I remember how cheerful, loud, and merry his voice sounded during his lessons with the children—and this despite his dreadful illness! A cheerful mood also reigned in his classroom. It's funny to me to think back to the frock coat with bright, shiny buttons that Uncle used to put on first thing in the morning for his lessons. A blond man with a small beard, he was short of stature, and so he always wore shoes with tall heels. The most handsome things about him were his intelligent, penetrating eyes and his broad forehead. I wouldn't say that Uncle Grigorii was an exceedingly kind man, but he was a very fair man, which is something I have always valued especially highly. This was his distinguishing characteristic.

For us children, life with Uncle was cozy and warm. Aunt treated us with great love, as if she were our own mother. But we children were not spoiled. Fortunately, parents in those days were less involved in raising children and therefore spoiled them less. After all, what do children need? To have full stomachs, to play to their heart's content, without any scolding, without constant reproof and admonishment—and in this manner they'll grow up to be normal, healthy people.

During the first year of our stay in Zakrochim, Uncle Grigorii himself taught us our lessons. These took place in the evenings, since he had no time during the day. I won't say that I liked our lessons. Every evening, when I was right in the middle of playing with the baker's children, I would hear my aunt calling me to hurry down from the cozy warmth of the stove for our cold and boring lessons. Under such unpleasant conditions, this seemed to me like a punishment, and I couldn't muster any particular enthusiasm for my studies.

What caused me the most trouble was having to read aloud the assigned lesson from the textbook every day. Uncle Grigorii required that we give a clear and exemplary recitation (we were taught in Russian), but I always read poorly; no matter how hard I tried, I would always stop short in the middle of the sentence. The fact of the matter was that we prepared our lessons by the light of a small kerosene lamp. I would stop after a minute's reading just to give my eyes a rest. This was very vexing for my uncle, but his scolding had no effect on me. Uncle Grigorii would assign me the same lesson over again, and I would cram for it (my sister would even help me), until I learned it by heart. Later, an eye doctor confirmed that I have dissimilar eyes, which is why when I read without glasses, the letters would blend together into one big pattern and the lines would float before my eyes.

Even today, children are blamed for much of what their instructors simply cannot understand. Unfortunate children! I deeply sympathize with you nowadays, and I'm sick at heart that we understand you so little, that we so undervalue your purity, your truthfulness, and your forgiving nature. Parents always think that they are right, because they are older. But they have too little respect for a child's personality, and they forget that if a child's upbringing doesn't go well, one needs to look for the causes—first and foremost—in the parents' incorrect approach to raising children. Such errors often hinder the development of the positive aspects of the child's personality for which nature has laid the foundations.

XII

Our life in Zakrochim passed quietly, without any great disturbances. Jews, Poles, and some Russians too lived together peacefully here, side by side. In this little town, the people were small, their affairs were small, their wages were small, and their needs were small, too. There were no shared, common interests; each person puttered about in his own little corner, busy with his own trifling, everyday concerns. This was particularly hard on the women. By the time evening came, after a whole day's work, our aunt would sit down to take a rest (for the first time all day), and during our lessons she'd fall fast asleep, right there at the table.

Men's work involved fewer tasks. Uncle Grigorii taught at the school and then had lessons with us, but his evening hours were dedicated to reading books and newspapers. I have fond memories of those evenings. After his rest at the end of the workday, Uncle Grigorii would emerge transformed. He was merry, told jokes, and especially loved to sing. In his side pocket he kept a thick little notebook with a fairly worn cover. He would write down his favorite songs in this little notebook, and over time it grew greatly in size. When he was in good humor, Uncle would sit me on his knee, and the two of us would sing together the whole evening long. In general, though, Uncle was strict with us. He would never give us permission, for example, to go with our neighbors to the woods and gather berries (the woods were five or six versts from our house). Our aunt tried to take advantage of those times when he was in a good mood to intercede on our behalf. Making fluttering eyes at Uncle, she would plead with him to let us skip our lessons and go for a stroll. We would hide around the corner so that we could overhear how the conversation turned out. For the most part, though, Uncle Grigorii would remain firm, and then our poor aunt would get frustrated and head off to bed early; we were sorrier for her than for ourselves.

To tell the truth, a stroll down to the woods was a wonderful treat for us. We would set out at five in the morning for the entire day, taking our food with us—bread with foxberries and cheese. Each of the children would fasten to themselves a piece of string, from which hung little tin cups of various sizes. After we'd gathered some bilberries, we would pour them from the small cups into the big one. We also had a big basket, where we kept all the berries we collected. It was not only fun, but useful, too. We would bring home a whole basket full of berries, and our aunt would make jam for the winter. Every day we would have bread with bilberry jam for second breakfast and a snack before dinner.

I remember that we used to dress very warmly. In those days, girls wore cotton pantaloons and wool petticoats in winter. Dressed this way, I spent many, many hours at our neighbor's, the baker's, beside the enormous stove, white-hot after a night of stoking the fires. Back then people were not very concerned with questions of hygiene, temperature, and diet. Strange as it may be, though, I don't recall that my sister and I ever fell ill.

Having guests over to Uncle Grigorii's house was out of the question—there was neither the time nor the means for this. But once in a while, a Polish fellow, a teacher at the public school, would stop by to see Uncle. This particular Pole was a real Pliushkin.[20] Uncle would play sixty-six with him, and you should have seen the look of distress on his face when he would tally up the total after the game and determine that he'd lost five or six kopecks![21] When sitting down to play, the Pole fully counted on winning. The money he made from playing cards was earmarked to buy a pair of shoes for his aged mother. The shoes cost two rubles and fifty kopecks. Over the course of the year, the beloved son would manage to save up enough money, but each time, right when he was about to purchase the shoes—a ten-kopeck loss! Uncle and Aunt would laugh heartily at their partner's losses. Meanwhile, over time, the gradual accumulation of such meager winnings began to add up.

Over the course of several years, Uncle Grigorii collected pieces of foil used for packaging tea. He took them from his friends, too, and then used them to plate our samovar. Such work required great patience, thoroughness, and a calm presence of mind.

There were no clocks in our house. Uncle had the only watch, and he carried it on his person. But our aunt had to know how many minutes it was before noon, so that she could start frying the onions and potatoes and prepare the celebrated beefsteak that she devoutly believed served as the foundation of Uncle Grigorii's strength, energy, and health. To this end, she would constantly send us off to find out what time it was. On a sunny day, we would run to the staircase and determine what time it was by the step on which the sunlight fell; on cloudy days we'd run down to the bakery and look at the clock.

Aside from games and studies, we occupied our time with handiwork—or at least I did, for by this time my sister was helping our aunt take care of her little baby. We would crochet doilies from thick, white thread. This was very painstaking work. Though I never did handiwork later in life, I was quite skilled at the time, and when I was in a groove I could turn out five or six of these patterns in a day. I would work without taking a break. Our aunt would use these patterns to cover the bed, the chest, and the table. These handmade patterns were the only decorations in our impoverished surroundings.

I mentioned that Uncle Grigorii had several acquaintances with whom he loved to talk politics. I remember one of them fondly. There were estates, farms, and woods surrounding Zakrochim. On one such estate there lived a retired general named Voronov. His country house was two versts from town. Almost every time he came into town, the general would call on Uncle, and the two of them would carry on long conversations together. My mission was to go to the general's house every day to pick up the newspaper *Golos*. Not a difficult task, but for a girl of eight, and a shy one at that (I have always been shy around people, not only as a child, but later in life as well), it was scary to set off on such a long journey. At the very last minute I would be overtaken with fear. I would approach the gate, push it open just the tiniest bit, and then slam it shut again—the furious dogs terrified me with their barking. And so it would continue until somebody appeared at the gate and walked me up to the house. Then, with a somewhat lighter heart, I headed for the general's study. All of the walls of the enormous room were lined with bookshelves; in a recess there stood a large sofa, and next to the windows overlooking the park, a colossal writing desk piled high with books and papers, where the master of the house worked. He was a tall, lean man with a gray head of hair, a little stooped, and so engrossed in his work that he would take notice of me only when I came up right beside him. I would stand close by, not yet having recovered from the fright and from my shyness. Once he noticed me, the general would greet me with a smile, pat me on the head, hand me the newspaper, and, without fail, treat me to a chocolate, saying: "All right then, go out to the garden and play with the children!" Then I'd forget my recent fears and race out to the middle of the garden, where there was a little playground for all sorts of different games. I particularly remember a very tall pole that we used as a rope swing. I would perch on the horizontal bar and grab onto the rope with my hands. The general's oldest son, who was already a young man (the general's family was very large), would give me a healthy kick, and I'd fly, as they say nowadays, off into the stratosphere, so that it took my breath away. At first I performed this little trick with a good deal of trepidation, but later I got used to it. I would play like this for an hour or so and then head home. The next day would be the very same—fear at first, then chocolate and games, and, finally, the walk home. I would return with a feeling of great joy and the sense of a job accomplished, never thinking that the very same ordeal awaited me the next day.

Uncle Grigorii knew nothing of what I went through. I loved and respected him very much, and I knew that I could not deprive him of the opportunity to read his newspaper. Once in a great while, Uncle would go to the general's house himself and take me with him. On those occasions I would think how easy, pleasant, and fun it was to go to the general's house with Uncle Grigorii, and how sad or, better yet, how frightening, it was to go alone! Uncle would remain in the general's study, and I would head straight to the garden, where the children were. After a long conversation, the two old gentlemen would come out to the garden, and we would have so much fun. After such a visit, Uncle and I would head home well satisfied, singing our favorite songs along the way.

I have only the foggiest memory of a certain Polish family with whom we were acquainted and who lived in a small country house. I recall the great celebration in this household, when the grandfather returned from many years in exile.[22] All his friends showed up to welcome him, and among them was our family. A whole crowd of people gathered together in one tiny room: we were treated to cakes, we drank and sang songs. I sat on the sofa, with my legs crossed beneath me, and gawked at the guests till I fell asleep.

Our neighbor the baker had a handful of kids, all of them very young. The oldest daughter, Maria, however, was already a typical Polish *panna*, cute and with a dimple in her chin.[23] She made clothes for the whole family, but on Saturdays she went dancing. Each of her girlfriends would take turns hosting a party every Saturday: this was the best way to hook a fiancé. Maria's best friend was Stasia. She was prettier, kinder, and, most importantly, more feminine than Maria, and therefore she was the first to find herself a fiancé—a young, handsome, and pleasant fellow. As such things go, the closer the friendship, the greater the jealousy. Our panna Maria was positively eaten up with envy, and she stopped going to the dances. Fury ill becomes a person, and Maria's charms soon faded. Her parents noticed this and tried to find a match for her.

Love is one thing—you grab the prettier one. Matchmaking is something else entirely—you grab the richer one. Life was bustling all around us, and though we children would gather round the stove and play our games without a care in the world, still we noticed things. A short, ugly man, already well along in years, with stubbly whiskers and a jacket that sat on him like a saddle on a cow, started calling on our panna Maria. We learned that this suitor had his own farm, that he had so many pigs, so many cows, and so forth. We didn't think anything special about this, but we would hide when he stopped by—we were afraid of his whiskers. Once I ran into him in the doorway. He bade farewell to his bride-to-be and kissed her gallantly on both hands, gazing into her eyes lovingly. She escorted him to the door with a sweet smile. Oh, but how her face changed the minute the door slammed shut behind him! Such anger and hate distorted her features! Shaking her fist at the departed fellow, she practically cried out in Polish: "The devil take you! Drop dead!" I stood there frozen and wide-eyed, but panna Maria, regaining her senses, shooed me from the room.

I recall yet another memorable event that has stayed with me my entire life. It took place at the beginning of the summer. It was terribly hot, and people were starting to head home after an evening spent in peaceful, quiet conversations on their porches. As always, my sister and I were lying down in our bed; I tried to press up against the wall so that I could put some room between my sister and me and have my own "living space," if you will.[24] Neither of us could fall asleep. Not half an hour had passed when there was a brilliant flash of lightning, followed by the sound of terrible rolls of thunder. The lightning blazed more and more frequently, the bolts grew larger and more jagged, the thunder bellowed uninterruptedly—it seemed as if the heavens had opened wide and that we would all be swallowed up in flames, that there was no hope of deliverance!

My sister and I lay there in great terror—I could feel that she was shaking all over; neither one of us could utter a single word from fear. We lived on the second floor, and the windows had no shutters or curtains—outside it was as bright as day! I squeezed my eyes shut so as not to see the flashes of lightning, when suddenly I heard the sound of our aunt's voice: "Children, you must be scared—get up!" Our whole bodies trembling, we jumped out of bed, hugged our aunt, and wept.

It turned out that Uncle and Aunt hadn't been able to sleep either, and they too were afraid to be left by themselves, so we all threw on some clothes and hurried downstairs to the bakery. And what did we find there? All our closest neighbors had also relocated to the bakery—Jews and Poles, everybody began to pray, each in his own fashion, that God would have mercy upon us and deliver us sinners from this misfortune. The children huddled close to the older folks and wept.

Everyone felt like passengers on a ship destined to go down. We sat there until five in the morning, waiting for death each minute. By that time, the thunder had begun to gradually die down, and all the people headed for their homes, tired and worn out, but happy to be left among the living. To this very day, whenever there is a big thunderstorm, I remember that terrible night in Zakrochim. People back then were more superstitious than they are now; they thought that the thunder was a punishment from God, and thus their fear was so great.

XIII

We lived in Zakrochim for about three years. By the last two years I was already attending school. This was a public school for girls: there was no special Jewish school in town. Our teacher was a Polish woman. The official language of instruction was Russian, but in fact we read and wrote primarily in Polish.

In my uncle's school, children's education came first and foremost, but not here. Neither the teacher nor the students were very much interested in ordinary lessons. I don't remember that we ever sang or played or made any noise at all during the morning hours: it was as if we were all serving out a long sentence. This wasn't the case, though, after lunch: then, children and teacher came together as one close-knit family. We were supposed to busy ourselves with handiwork after lunch, but we chatted instead. Our teacher would sit atop the table, leaning her legs against the chair (I copied this manner of sitting years later when I was in charge of the public school in Bobruisk), and we would sit at our desks, and this way she could see all the children in front of her and focus her attention on them; at times like this it seemed to us that she was up on a pedestal.

Our teacher was young and beautiful, and it seemed to me that she had about her some sort of special, otherworldly beauty; she was modest and quiet, with a lively look in her eyes, and a voice that was soft and tender to the ear. I was captivated by her. After lunch, she wouldn't bother maintaining strict order in the classroom or giving us lessons; we sat spellbound, listening to her stories about Christ, of his love for people, for humanity, for children in particular, and for all the oppressed and downtrodden. We listened to her, holding our breath, admiring her pretty face, experiencing together with her the sufferings of Christ. After she had fallen silent, we would sit still for a long time without moving: it was hard to make the transition back from the heavens to the everyday.

The daily sermon concluded with the class kneeling in common prayer. I was the only Jew and I didn't kneel, but in my heart I prayed together with the others. I knew all the prayers, of course, by heart. Then, after having kissed our teacher's hand, we headed home without a sound. To me, kissing our teacher's hand was a real sacred act: she seemed to me a being who stood at some unattainable height. I passionately believed that she was no ordinary earthly being, but a messenger of Christ, sent down to earth to sow good among children.

Once I met her in the woods during a walk. I had been gathering berries and didn't notice that I had become separated from the others, and so I found myself completely alone in a green thicket. For a long time I just wandered to and fro, pouring berries from one cup into another. And whom should I suddenly see there? My beloved teacher, on her knees, praying; her sister, who suffered from a nervous condition, sat nearby on the grass. I froze and did not move from where I stood, for fear of interrupting her direct, unmediated communion with God. I even imagined that I saw delicate wings on her shoulders. It occurred to me that her mission in life was not an easy one, and that was why her face always bore such an expression of suffering. When she finished her prayer, she must have taken note of my admiring gaze, for she came up to me and stroked my head. I kissed her hand. Then she helped me find the others. But I could no longer gather berries with the same passion as before: I was preoccupied with different thoughts.

From that moment on, I often found myself lost in thought. There was no time for this during the day, what with school and games, but in the evenings, lying there in my half of the bed, pressed up against the wall, I would give myself over to my thoughts. About what? About going off to join a monastery. There, it seemed to me, I would be nearer to God and could live in a godly fashion. What I understood by these words is hard to tell.

I remember once, while out on a stroll with my aunt and uncle, we walked past the monastery. There at the gate stood a Jewish boy, who had run away from home. The Jews who walked by cursed him loudly, but I envied him.[25] It goes without saying that I said not a single word to my uncle of what I was then feeling or thinking. Ever since, I've always liked to have a little secret corner of my own where I can think my thoughts in seclusion.

No one at home had any idea about our teacher's conversations with us, and still less about my "plans." And right at the very height of all this, as I stood on the verge, as it seemed, of realizing my hazy plans, a great change took place in my life. One day, when I was playing with the baker's children, I was called home and hurriedly told to put on my wool clothing, in two layers. My father had sent instructions from Siberia that Uncle Grigorii was to take us to Plotsk, where there was a gymnasium; we were to live there with Uncle Avraam. And thus, without any warning, I was torn away from everything near, dear, and familiar to me. We were loaded up into the buda, while our aunt wept, welling up with tears. With her loving heart, she sensed that life would not be so warm for us in Plotsk, that there we would be just another pair of boarding students lodged at Uncle Avraam's.

Farewell, dear, quiet, peaceful, idyllic Zakrochim! We go off into the wide, uncharted world, where we will be just a couple of countless grains of sand. What will become of us? Who will take care of us now?

XIV

Strange as it sounds, I have almost no memory of the journey to Uncle Avraam's. Everything took place, as it were, in a fog, and it was difficult to make sense of what was happening. The general impression at the time was that we had left behind a warm and cozy family home where we were surrounded by loving people, and had wound up in some sort of institution—although a well-appointed one, to be sure. No one embraced us, no one stroked our heads, no one spoke so much as a single kind word.

We weren't much to look at, in our cotton-wool skirts and jackets, wearing head scarfs, which, as I recall, we had used from time to time as handkerchiefs to blow our noses. What's more, I was terribly shy around people. I looked everywhere for a place to hide and held tight to my sister, as if to an anchor, to save me.

All of this, plus the multitude of new faces around us—these are my impressions from the first few weeks of my stay in Plotsk. Uncle Avraam and Aunt Ol'ga made no effort to get to know us, to understand our individual psyches: we were simply numbered among the general ranks of the boarding students. These were students from prosperous families in Plotsk, Warsaw, and Lodz, students who had difficulties in their studies or, more likely, who had been poorly taught and received Ds and Fs in school. They were sent here because Uncle Avraam was considered to be a good pedagogue and, moreover, because he had connections among the local teachers. He was a teacher of Jewish scripture in the local gymnasium. In the evenings, Uncle Avraam graded the children's lessons, demanding that their assignments be completed diligently. Besides the two of us, there were six or seven boarding students.

Being a very sociable person, my sister adjusted more quickly and easily than I to our new surroundings. She made friends right away with Uncle Avraam's oldest daughter, even though she was three years older than my sister. Meanwhile, I moped and fretted about the house. Uncle Avraam prepared us both for the gymnasium. He was a very educated man for those days. When he was already married with two children, he had left his family behind and gone off to Zhitomir to enter the Teachers Institute. It must not have been easy for him to do this—in addition to his own studies, he was obliged to offer lessons for mere pennies in order to survive. His wife and children remained with her parents, somewhere in Poland.

In later years, Uncle Avraam recounted the events of his life. I remember how he wrote his autobiography in Kuchkuryshka outside Vil'na, where the owners of the paper factory (which included members of our family) had lived for decades. In 1910, Uncle went there for the summer to stay with his brother, our father. I remember that he read several chapters from his autobiography aloud to us.[26] Uncle Avraam was a modest and delicate man, noble but completely unprepossessing. He was a man not made for this world, and he appeared utterly helpless when it came to matters of everyday life. He constantly fiddled around with his books, reading and writing during the long winter evenings, long past midnight, after an exhausting day of work. As a literary critic, he contributed to various Jewish journals. In Plotsk, he enjoyed particular esteem among broad circles of society, and in the teaching community as well. Every teacher at the gymnasium considered it his duty to call on Uncle Avraam on Jewish holidays and offer his best wishes; every new colleague called on him for a visit.

Like the majority of Jewish writers at the time, Uncle Avraam wrote his articles in Russian. Only in later years, after the first Russian revolution, did Jewish writers recognize the importance of the language in which the popular masses spoke. On a certain occasion, after the Revolution of 1905, Uncle Avraam was in Petersburg for a banquet held in his honor by Jewish writers. There he made a public apology (though perhaps not, as some said, with tears in his eyes), saying that for the greater part of his life he had written in a language foreign to the Jewish masses.

As the reader can see, the two brothers, my uncles, had much in common. But our aunts, who were not related by birth, were complete opposites. Our aunt in Zakrochim reminded me of a village woman who worked from sunup to sundown and made no fuss over her outward appearance. On the other hand, Uncle Avraam's wife, Aunt Ol'ga, had all the mannerisms of a high-society city lady who had found herself among the middle classes. At the time, Uncle already had four children. It was not easy to support such a large family on a civil servant's modest wages, but fortunately nature had granted Aunt Ol'ga that which Uncle lacked—a practical turn of mind. And how! She decided to make use of Uncle Avraam's only talents that could yield practical results. He was renowned as a good pedagogue and educator, and so Aunt Ol'ga began to take in boarding students, receiving a tidy little sum for their tuition and room and board. Every evening Uncle Avraam was obliged to teach children who fell into one of two categories: those who were capable but lazy, and those who were genuinely stupid or nearly retarded. The work was pure drudgery, yet Uncle Avraam still found time for his literary efforts; at least he could pour his soul into this work.

We lived with Uncle Avraam for two years. Not once during this whole time did I manage to get close to him, and not once did he turn to us, his own flesh and blood, with a warm word. He spent all his time by himself, in his bedroom, where he read, wrote, and taught his students. He took interest in us only at first; afterward, we were educated like everyone else and no longer needed his help. Uncle Avraam had a handsome face with well-proportioned features; he had large side-whiskers, that is, he shaved only the middle of his chin; it seems that all teachers back then were expected to wear side-whiskers. He was very short as well.

I remember how later on, in Vil'na, our stepmother would always reproach Father for Uncle Avraam's short stature. When someone from the younger generation would stop growing, she would always say: "Oh, that Avraam of yours. He only comes up to *here* on me," and thereupon she would point to the back of her head, "and wait, you'll see, our daughter Idochka will grow up to be just as tiny as Avraam." Then she would sigh—half seriously and half in jest. Hearing this, our Papasha would guiltily slink away.

XV

It was very crowded for us to live with Uncle Avraam; it seems that each of us was allotted no more "living space" than they are nowadays in Soviet Russia. The apartment consisted of four connected rooms without hallways. Beds were set up in all the rooms. One room was set aside for the boys, another for the girls. There was also a bedroom for Aunt Ol'ga and Uncle Avraam, where their little kids slept, too, and a dining room, where their older children slept. Since there was not enough room downstairs for all the boarding students, Aunt Ol'ga set up a little attic room at the top of the staircase: three girls were lodged up there, including me. I remember one of the other girls was the daughter of the well-known Lodz manufacturer Poznanski.[27]

Here, too, as in Bobruisk and Zakrochim, I had to sleep two to a bed. What a cruel joke of fate! Ever since childhood, I have suffered from having to be too close to other people—I could not bear anyone touching my body; my girlfriends in gymnasium called me Princess Touch-Me-Not, because I did not like to kiss. We lived our own life in that upstairs room. To put it more accurately, we lived vicariously by spying on the lives of the older boys and girls.

In general, Uncle Avraam and Aunt Ol'ga divided the duties at the boarding school between themselves. Uncle's responsibilities consisted of instruction in the classroom, as well as the development of students' minds (as much as it was possible, of course). Aunt Ol'ga took upon herself instruction in etiquette, primarily the cultivation of good manners, especially as it pertained to the girls. The boys paid very little attention to her. They held Uncle Avraam in very high esteem, however, and he did have some influence on them. But living in that house and in that environment proved to be a stronger influence on them than Uncle Avraam—so I think now, at least.

What was life like at the boarding school? The very term *boarding school* gives you the answer: there was no talk of family togetherness, of heartfelt ties between people. Each boarder lived only for his own selfish interests, knowing full well that it was a tidy sum of money that paid for his food and schooling. According to Aunt Ol'ga, good upbringing consisted of being *zierlich-manierlich*,[28] especially the girls. For example, if one of us girls needed a notebook, it was considered unseemly to go out and fetch one all by ourselves. Instead, Aunt Ol'ga would summon the cook, who in the twinkling of an eye would be transformed into a household maid to accompany the boarder on her mission and parade ceremoniously behind her. Once out in the street, a girl would try to prolong the walk as much as possible— perhaps she'd meet a boy student from the gymnasium who might cast a furtive, but meaningful, glance in her direction. Incidentally, the maid, of course, was supposed to carry the purchased notebook.

When we were not busy with our studies, however, we were allowed to go out into the courtyard all by ourselves and get some fresh air. The courtyard, I remember, was large. Behind the enormous shed at the end of the courtyard, there was a cozy little playground, which looked out onto the Vistula River. We younger children used this spot as a place for jumping rope. I remember how we'd jump rope until we wore ourselves out. The older boarding students also really loved this spot: the girls from the gymnasium would have rendezvous here with local gymnasium boys. Our neighbor, a beautiful artist, also arranged meetings here with the officers who courted her. These meetings took place, of course, not in the daytime, when children played there, but in the evenings—"at the gray hour," to use the Polish phrase. Still, we knew all about them.

The fact of the matter was that our little attic room served as a nice observation deck: crouching down on your knees beside the window and leaning forward a little bit, you could see everything that was taking place on the playground. I must admit, our favorite pastime was peeping and spying on kissing couples rotating in and out, just like images in a kaleidoscope. We roomed upstairs, you see, without any supervision. I can imagine how horrified Auntie Ol'ga would have been, had she discovered how we passed the time!

Our day was strictly regimented: school, meals, preparing for lessons—all under the supervision of the senior students. Uncle Avraam's oldest daughter, who had already completed the gymnasium and was helping her mother around the house, kept track of the girls' lessons. After a whole day spent downstairs, we were excited to be dismissed to go upstairs after supper. We were supposed to go to bed immediately, and the servant checked up on us. Obediently, we undressed and got into bed, and the servant left, taking the candle with her. We didn't do as we were told, however—children aren't just mannequins. We managed to "bend the rules," of course, having asked the neighbor's servant to buy a couple of tallow candles. Our little rich girl, Poznanski's daughter, put up the money for the candles. Incidentally, I never had any pocket money of my own—not only in childhood, but in later years as well, not until I went off to take courses in Petersburg. I never felt that I needed money.

In any event, the idea proved superb: we had our own source of light, and it never occurred to Aunt to make sure that we were sleeping. I don't recall exactly how we spent those evenings—we must have had as much fun as we knew how. Sometimes, though, we'd get drawn into more "serious" pursuits: thanks to watching out the window, Poznanska and I had picked up a little bit of the ways of the world, and so we'd try our hand at literary efforts. We had all the necessary items for this, you see: an attic, a tallow candle, and life experience!

And so without having agreed on it beforehand, we all of a sudden began writing poems simultaneously. The canvas was already at hand—the courting of gymnasium girls by gymnasium boys—all that remained was to embroider the pattern. I remember how we would work on our poems till long after midnight, both of us lying in that single bed, excited by everything that we had just seen not so long before. The fruit of our labors was a satirical poem. I won't say that the work came easy to us—we labored over it, one line after another, till the break of dawn. We wrote in Polish, because we spoke Russian with no one in Plotsk except for Uncle Avraam. Out of that whole poem I remember only one excerpt:

Students in higher grades,
With moustaches and beards,
Change their ties
Twice a week,
They powder their faces
And wear white gloves,
But still they look
Like monkeys!

We included a lot of irony and contempt for the male sex in this satire. We were at the age when antagonism between girls and boys is at its very height; then begins the opposite phenomenon—secret adoration.

Even with the help of a servant, it was not easy for Aunt Ol'ga to deal with a gang of kids in such cramped quarters. She had no small amount of work to do herself, what with making sure she bought enough food to feed everyone without overspending. She would bustle about from early in the morning till late in the evening, though without ever losing her robust figure and aristocratic mannerisms. On big holidays or family celebrations, Aunt and Uncle would set off on their visits. Uncle Avraam would have rather used the free evening for his literary efforts, but Aunt Ol'ga was in charge of the ceremony of visiting, and so the poor man, whether he wanted to or not, had to put on a clean collar and a white tie and don his new frock coat (throughout his entire life he probably had only the same two frock coats: one was considered "new," the other "old"). Our aunt would completely transform herself: her hair teased up; her cheeks powdered; her shoulders raised up with an air of self-importance, she walked with the carriage of a queen. Across her shoulders she threw an old lace cape (much worn, the entire thing was darned and patched up), which served her faithfully and truly on all formal occasions throughout her long life.

Aunt Ol'ga was an intelligent woman, a woman of the world; she knew when to smile graciously, and when to get by with only a haughty nod of the head. During their visits, Uncle Avraam faded into the background a bit; he gladly yielded the spotlight to his wife and dreamed of only one thing: serving out his time as quickly as possible and returning home to his beloved books. These two people, so unlike each other, lived a long life together, peacefully and amicably; such marriages were rare in those days.

I still have not yet spoken of the town where we lived. As far as I can remember, Plotsk was a handsome town, even by today's standards. The streets were all paved, the houses were made of stone, none taller than two stories, and there were many parks and town squares. Especially scenic was the embankment on the Vistula, alongside the park, where there was music on Sundays. Sometimes we strolled in the park under the watchful eye of Auntie Ol'ga, who stepped out proudly in her famous cape and her hat with a small ostrich feather (not much to look at) sticking straight up. We would promenade down the embankment two by two, as befitting young girls from an "aristocratic" boarding school.

Our stay in Plotsk came to an end unexpectedly, just as in Zakrochim. Once again, instructions came from Father, this time not from Siberia but from Vil'na. Our father had married for a second time and had settled down in Vil'na. Without any tears, without any touching farewells, our things were dutifully packed in a small basket, and we left Plotsk, anxiously wondering, Where are we going and what is waiting for us?

Before our departure, Sister asked Uncle Avraam to write something in her scrapbook to remember him by. He was a little surprised and embarrassed, but he took the little book and jotted down this long, rhythmic bon voyage, which seems quite naive to me today:

You ask of me,
My child dear,
A few words of farewell.
Here, then, is my last testament to you:
Be smart, but listen always
To those who are smarter than you.
Be proud,
For pride is like a necklace on a young girl,
But not always:
Oftentimes she must be modest . . .

The farewell poem was long, but I can remember only these lines.

C H A P T E R   T W O

Gymnasium Years

(Vil'na, 1880–85)

I

From the age of thirteen to sixteen, the life of a teenage girl is a period of uncertainty, fogginess, vague aspirations, and hazy dreaming. A young creature can often lose her way in this labyrinth. Nevertheless, most people of my generation grew into conscious, self-aware people with defined tastes and preferences, people who had found their place in life. Youth is the most difficult and dangerous time in one's life, and a young girl has nowhere to turn for help and support. Unfortunately, this is the period least studied by psychologists. Educators do not stop to think about what chaos governs the souls of young people and how hard it is for them to understand the world around them. A chance meeting with a companion, be it good or bad, may prove to be a decisive one and may determine a young person's entire fate. For it is from individuals that all humanity is composed!

When I left for Vil'na, I was around twelve years old. This was the third, and final, stage of our family's journeys. Henceforth, Vil'na would become our permanent home. Even though I would leave for long periods of time, even for whole years, in the end I would always return to this city, where I live now and where, most likely, I will end this mortal life.

As I've mentioned before, my sister and I were complete opposites. The difference in our characters was apparent in our attitudes toward Vil'na. My sister always maintained that she never felt so at ease as she did in Vil'na. I myself, however, never harbored any particular attachment to the place; I was always drawn to the big city—"to Moscow, to Moscow!"[1] It's given me no little grief that the greater portion of my life has been spent in the provinces, but you can't escape your fate, as they say. I must confess, however, that I'm the cause of this, having condemned myself to a fourteen-year sentence in the swamps of Bobruisk, which lie adjacent to the somewhat more celebrated swamps of Pinsk.[2]

In Zakrochim, as in Plotsk, we lived outside the Jewish world. With our arrival in Vil'na, however, we once again found ourselves in the very heart of Jewish life and culture. Father at that time was not quite forty years of age, but a decade spent in Siberia, in a purely Russian environment, had left its mark on his outward appearance. They had even given him a Russian name out there, one which had nothing whatsoever in common with his real name: instead of Faitel', they "christened" him Pavel (thus, I am Anna Pavlovna) and gave him a suitable patronymic as well—Semënovich. In Siberia, my father associated with engineers, merchants, and all sorts of colleagues who worked in the gold mines. On account of his work, Father often had to travel through thick forests; he would journey many hundreds of versts into the woods and even took part in bear hunts on more than one occasion. Though ordinarily not a garrulous man, Father could spend hours telling us about his life in Siberia, about his various adventures, about the time he traveled to Irkutsk to spend Christmas in the home of some wealthy merchants, and so on. Father felt very much at ease in Siberia, even though the Bobruisk heder where he received his education could not have prepared him for life in Siberia.

Now, as I write these lines, I am reminded of the words of Delianov, with whom I pleaded to allow my brother to return to university.[3] He stared at me for a long time, and then, enunciating each syllable, he said: "The most remarkable characteristic of your nationality is your ex-traor-di-nary persistence!" To paraphrase Delianov, but with a slight alteration: our most remarkable characteristic is our extraordinary adaptability! No wonder that in Siberia Papasha transformed himself into Pavel Semënovich. Outwardly, Father bore little resemblance to a Jew. Nature had endowed him with fair hair, blue eyes, and a nose that was short but broad, like Tolstoy's. He said little and spoke quietly, and was cordial in his dealings with others.

Thanks to his second marriage, my father found himself in an environment that was the complete opposite of his Siberian surroundings. Father's wife—our stepmother, Mamasha—was at that time thirty-five years old. She had three sons from her first husband, who died young—the oldest boy was twelve or thirteen, the youngest eight. The youngest bore his father's first name and later acquired a reputation in Vil'na as a doctor and a public figure. This was Dr. Makover.[4] Mamasha was her parents' only daughter. They owned a general store on Bol'shaia Street, which was quite large for its time. They seemed ancient to me, although the old woman was only seventeen years older than her daughter.

We traveled to Vil'na with Uncle Avraam. Our father was then living on Sirotskaia Street, in the house of Dr. Trakhtenberg. There was a steep staircase in the middle of the house, which led to a long corridor where there were two apartments: our stepmother's parents lived in one, consisting of two rooms and a kitchen; we lived in the other, which had four rooms. We all shared the kitchen.

Vil'na—the third stage on our journey. I'd grown three years older with each new stop along the way, but my impressions got hazier as I grew older: our arrival in Zakrochim is still vivid in my memory; our arrival in Plotsk comes to me in a haze, as if through a fog; and of our arrival in Vil'na I remember not a thing. Apparently the impressions of early childhood—at any rate, those which have lodged in one's memory, for whatever reason—stand out for their extraordinary clarity.

II

In Vil'na we found ourselves in a completely unfamiliar environment. I had no memory of Father whatsoever: we had not received a single letter from him throughout our long separation. Thanks to her easygoing nature, my sister quickly became accustomed to the new situation and made friends not only with Mamasha, but even with Mamasha's mother, who really took a liking to my sister and often invited her over for a cup of tea. As for me, I became even more shy and avoided people. Like a snail, I constantly withdrew into my shell, only rarely sticking my head out. Mamasha was very sensible and right away took upon herself all concerns for our well-being, thereby freeing Father from any sort of obligations toward us. Like Grandfather, our father was a very self-centered man—he eagerly handed us over to Mamasha's care straightaway, without our really even knowing her, and without taking into account the difficulties of our living situation. Now as before, living together under the same roof, my father and I shared absolutely nothing in common. I instinctively felt complete apathy toward him.

I maintained very proper relations with Mamasha, but no more than that. I kept to myself from the very beginning. I made no demands on my father or stepmother but was rewarded all the same by the particular attentiveness and love that my sister showed me. Mamasha's father was quite a bit older than his wife, perhaps fifteen years or more. His children from his first marriage were all dead, and Mamasha was the only child from his second marriage. He loved her deeply and showed her far more tenderness than he did her mother. Judging from my sister's stories, the couple's married life was not a very happy one.

The old man's outward appearance was not much to look at. Short, thin, with a curly head of hair that had never known a comb, and a disheveled beard, he looked eternally embittered. His wife was significantly younger, a beautiful and practical woman, always impeccably dressed and full of life. She was cold toward her daughter, perhaps because she had never loved her husband. Both of them were extraordinarily devout; compared to them, Grandfather was a freethinker. And this is the family in which our father—the "goy" Pavel Semënovich—now found himself! Fortunately, Mamasha had already been touched by civilization. She was distinguished by her natural gifts, a purely masculine mind, and her extensive reading (of course, she was self-taught).

Mamasha was particularly fond of the German classics. Thanks to her colossal memory, she could recite whole passages from Goethe and Heine, but her true love was Lessing. It seems she derived her entire store of wisdom from *Nathan the Wise*.[5] Mamasha loved to discuss philosophy, and she impressed everyone around her—people called her "the wise one." Later on, in Switzerland, when my parents met Natanson (the well-known Socialist Revolutionary), he was delighted at Mamasha's mind and at the breadth of her views.[6]

Friction between parents and children is a common thing, and our family was no exception. The old folks tried to retain their role as educators of the young: they recognized no schooling but the heder. But now in her second marriage, Mamasha had begun to share my father's point of view, that it was necessary to give children a secular education. It was over this very issue that arguments and bad feelings broke out between my parents and the old folks. The principal argument that Mamasha's parents put forward against secular education was that children should not be required to write on the Sabbath. In the end, however, it was the younger generation who carried the day: Mamasha's eldest boy enrolled in the *Realschule*, and the two younger children continued for now at the heder.[7] The boy lived with his grandfather and grandmother; the old folks had to settle for him laying on the *tefillin* and praying for a long time before setting out for school.[8] As it happened, the boy would wake up late and seldom was able to say his prayers. When she saw that he had started eating without having prayed, his grandmother would shout at him from the other room: "May you choke on your breakfast!"

The harmony did not last long, however: two years later, the old man fell very ill. Mamasha was abroad at the time, at Reichenhall, perhaps.[9] The sick man's condition got worse by the day. He realized the peril of his situation and was deeply distressed that his beloved only daughter was not by his side. When he was healthy, he had always harbored a certain malice toward his wife—perhaps he envied her youth. But during his sickness this feeling grew even more pronounced, and only rarely would he allow her to come in and see him; he probably sensed that deep down she would be glad to be rid of him. When things took a sharp turn for the worse, the sick man demanded that his daughter be called for. Mamasha set out at once, but the journey took a full day and night. I remember the precise moment of her arrival. The sick man had gone through some torturous moments, battling with death, as if trying to delay its onset. In the final hours of his life, he opened his eyes with great effort and asked whether Khana had arrived. All this time he held a set of keys tightly gripped in his hands—they must have been for the cash register, he entrusted them to no one. Finally, at midnight, dressed all in black and in a black hat, as if she had had a premonition of his death, Mamasha ran into the room and threw herself upon her dying father. I was standing in the shadows of the room and saw everything. The sick man hoisted himself up with supernatural strength, opened his arms into a wide embrace, pressed his daughter to his breast, and, as if he were satisfied, lowered himself back down onto the pillow, stretched out . . . and let out his last breath.

The old man's death brought with it practically no changes in the lives of those near to him. His wife was then forty-six or forty-seven years old. My father took his place behind the cash register, and all of the old man's business affairs—buying goods in Moscow and selling them in town—were handled by his widow and Mamasha, as before.

III

In those days, the store opened at seven o'clock in the morning and closed at eleven o'clock at night. My parents devoted about an hour to lunch, plus a walk afterward. The salesgirls, young girls and some married women, worked without a break. They brought their lunch from home and swiftly scoffed it down while leaning over the counter. If a customer came in during lunch and requested the service of a particular salesgirl, she would put down her food right away and with redoubled zeal, as it were, display the goods in a persuasive and ingratiating manner, all the while swearing up and down that it was impossible to sell the items any cheaper. These sales pitches always seemed to irritate my father.

At night, exhausted and worn out (having not sat down once the entire day; indeed, there was nowhere to sit down), the salesgirls slumbered, resting their heads on a few scraps of cloth. Hard work, however, did not prevent the married girls from having lots of kids. One of the salesgirls, Dveira, had eight children and loved them all equally. In her youth she had been a great beauty and married a Torah scribe who earned a pittance. Their principal means of support were the three rubles a week that Dveira received for her labors. Our salesgirls were wholly devoted to their households, even to the point of self-sacrifice.

Mamasha's mother, now a widow, did not long outlive her husband. About a year after his death, she fell ill with nephritis. We were all in the city at the time, while Mamasha alone stayed with her sick mother at the dacha.[10] She had the difficult task of tending to the sick woman for many months, but her energy and selfless devotion, far from waning, seemed to grow stronger by the day. Mamasha did not get a full night's sleep for the duration of her mother's illness, and she grew so accustomed to going without sleep that she suffered from insomnia for a long time to come. At the end of the summer, the sick woman passed away.

IV

Back in Vil'na, a family council was held to decide the fate of me and my sister. It was resolved that in the fall I would take the entrance examination for the gymnasium. Since my sister was taller and more developed, our parents decided not to send her off to school: let her grow up a little bit more, and then it would be time for her to marry. A schoolteacher was hired to give me lessons—she taught in the same gymnasium I was preparing to enter. She was paid, I think, thirty rubles a month, which was quite a lot in those days. It is possible that this was a bribe of sorts, since passing the exams was guaranteed in advance.

One of the examinations I was required to take was in Orthodox Christian theology. I gave a short answer to our teacher's question— Who was the first man?—but could say no more. The teacher then started asking me about Uncle Avraam and wound up giving me an A instead of an F. People usually think that it's only their rich relatives who can help them out in life, but this time it was my poor uncle!

I entered the fourth class of a seven-class gymnasium. It's not worth going into much detail concerning our gymnasium. The teaching was conventional, the knowledge trifling. Even over a period of seven years, students still didn't manage to complete the course in arithmetic! We divided the teachers into those we hated, those we liked, and those we simply adored. One teacher in particular was especially popular. He was indeed a handsome man, and every single one of the girls had a crush on him. One of the girls just so happened to meet this teacher on the street one day, and the next day the entire class was green with envy toward the lucky girl. She felt obliged to go on and on in great detail (I think the tale became more colorful with each telling) about how she was dumbstruck when she first ran into him, how she regained her composure and managed to curtsey, and how he responded with a cordial nod of the head. Huddled in a circle, choked up with emotion, we listened to her tale for what must have been the tenth time.

It turned out that there were less pleasant encounters as well. Once, during a lengthy break between classes, our principal spotted me in one of the classrooms. Our principal was a pedant, a nasty woman with sadistic tendencies, and she dragged me by the sleeve to the teachers' common room, where all the teachers were gathered. I was taken aback: true, I wasn't one of the "Goody Two-shoes," but I didn't feel I had done anything wrong. Her face all twisted, she shoved me into the common room and showed me to my teacher, who was flirting with the handsome instructor (later on, they were married). Stammering with rage, she hissed: "Look at her, look. She . . . she's . . . without her bow!" Each class had to wear a specific colored bow, which was fastened to our white collar, but I had forgotten to wear it! The teachers looked at the criminal and smiled gently, and I quickly hopped out into the hallway. The principal also required that we wear galoshes year-round. But once we got to school, we put our galoshes in a sack, hung them up with our overcoats, and then carried them home at the end of the day. We were quite pleased with our little trick, but the old witch wanted us to obey.

I was an average student. Our classroom had six rows of desks, and where we were seated depended on how successful we were in our studies. I was seated always in the third row. There were some real natural-born scholars in our class, who competed among themselves. Far from envying them, we average students treated them with scorn and considered them mere memorizers who studied only to get good grades. We students in the older classes had already read Belinskii and Pisarev, and engaged in discussions on all sorts of elevated themes. We even read Chernyshevskii's *What Is to Be Done?* We were drawn to the forbidden.[11]

During these years I was very anemic and suffered from loss of appetite—it was not uncommon for me to feel sick at the mere sight of food. I left for school every morning on an empty stomach, and along the way I would stop at the bakery and buy two biscuit cookies for three kopecks, although I would eat only one of them. I often felt light-headed, and as soon as I arrived home from school, I would fling my bag aside and lie down in bed, without even undressing. Our room was on the other side of the partition, behind the dining room, without much light. There were two beds and two chairs; there was a cot, too—I can see it now—which was always covered with white paper. There was no table, so I kept my books on the cot. I spent the greater part of the day in the other room—a brightly lit child's room, which Mamasha's young son shared with Idochka, the daughter from her marriage with Father. I will return to this exceptional girl in due course; she was fated to have a tragic life and an even more tragic death while in the very flower of life.[12]

I never prepared for my lessons. I would cram for exams on the way from one class to another. Strange as it seems, though, I studied hard during the exam period, even with enthusiasm, and earned Bs. The main incentive for working hard in school was the fear of having to repeat a grade and thereby having to part with one's classmates. Once, before final exams, my health took a sharp turn for the worse, and the military doctor who treated me categorically insisted that I depart for Switzerland at once, for a year or two. I dug in my heels and declared that I'd rather die than repeat a grade. During one's youth, one knows nothing of the value of life and does not fear death. "I'll take my exams early," I repeated, "and then I'll be ready for whatever happens . . ." I was then seventeen years old.

I was very tall for my age and flat-chested and must have looked funny in the short dress that the second-year girls wore—it barely reached my knees. I didn't pay any particular attention to this, but my girlfriends insisted on sewing a longer dress for me in time for final exams. I owned no other dresses at the time. Exams came and my nerves were strained to the breaking point, so the doctor treated me with new methods—the cupping and the leeches were abandoned, and I started taking arsenic.[13] Then a miracle happened—despite my nervous strain during the exam period, I began to recover. My cheeks reddened, I put on weight, I became more lively and energetic, my light-headedness disappeared, and I became a healthy young girl.

V

After the old folks died, my parents had to move to a new apartment. We lived on Kazimirskii Lane. There were only two houses on our little road—across the way there stretched the high wall of the bishop's residence, on Bol'shaia Street. Despite some major shortcomings, our apartment gave the appearance of a gentleman's manor house. A wide staircase led upward; the foyer was large, square, and bright; and wide redwood doors with multicolored glass panels led to a large study with a corner window. To the right was the drawing room, with two windows that opened out onto the dark little lane, opposite a blank wall. Past the study was a rather plain dining room, and next to it a small bright room that my sister and I shared. Our little sister, Idochka, slept in our parents' bed. The boys were assigned a large common room, and next door, in the storage closet, lodged one of Mamasha's distant relatives—a poor orphan girl. Her name was Basia. She sat at the sewing machine constantly, sewing and mending for the entire family and weeping bitterly for days on end at her sad orphan's fate. At first we lived very modestly indeed: our parents rented out one room to Mamasha's cousin, who had graduated from a polytechnic institute in Riga and taken a position in one of the Jewish banks in Vil'na. He lived with us for two years.

In the new apartment, our life took on a different cast: there was no more terror visited on us from pious elders, no more morning prayers, no more stormy scenes over whether someone had used the wrong knife or fork, no more having to go to synagogue on the Sabbath. We gradually became "Europeanized." My sister played a large part in this transformation. Mamasha was a busy woman and gladly handed over to Sister the reins of government, that is to say, the management of the household. Sister notified Mamasha of her plans for household reform, and each time Mamasha would usually respond merrily in Yiddish: "Ah, gladly." And so with all the ardor of youth, my sister set about restructuring our lives. Just like Peter the Great! The older boys already attended public school and wore proper uniforms, and so the first victim of the reforms was our younger brother. My sister ordered him a little suit, consisting of short pants and a sailor's blouse (instead of long trousers and a jacket). No matter how much he protested that he didn't want to look like a little kid, it was no use: my sister was the supreme authority. There was only one innovation that she was unable to implement. Of course, one needed a matching cap to go with the sailor's blouse, and so my sister bought a white cap with a blue ribbon running all the way around. To avoid any unnecessary discussion of the matter, she simply hid our little brother's old, peaked cap. But our brother showed stiff resistance. In the morning, seeing the caps were switched, he started kicking and screaming in protest. Mamasha had to intervene, and, in the end, the poor boy, suppressing his indignation, set off for the old-fashioned heder in his new, stylish cap. But my sister did not have long to rejoice. A few days afterward, our brother categorically declared that he would no longer go to heder in this ridiculous outfit, nor indeed anywhere at all (his friends must have made fun of him). Seeing how angry he was, my sister was forced finally to relent.

At that time I displayed no artistic talents and had little interest in the household furnishings and all the goings-on that were part of family life. No matter, though, for my sister played an active part in keeping our home comfortable. Incidentally, in those days aesthetic needs were quite primitive. I still remember the furniture in our dining room—a ridiculously large sideboard and table, some uncomfortable chairs, and two prints that Father had purchased. These hung on opposite sides of the enormous sideboard. One had the caption, "Before the hunt," and showed the hunter sitting at the table, drinking merrily in anticipation of the day's quarry. The other read, "After the hunt," with the same man sitting gloomily at the table, his head hung low and an empty game-sack in his hands. These were the very first pictures I had seen in my life.

VI

My sister dressed quite simply. She had only two outfits to wear in every season: last year's outfit and a newer one. These were long, seamless dresses, so long they practically had trains; on top, she wore jackets made of the same material, and capes with short sleeves. One of these outfits, I recall, was a chocolate brown, trimmed with tan velvet. My sister wore high starched collars—the ends were turned up in front, revealing a bit of décolletage. A wide satin ribbon wound around the collar, fastening in the front with a large bow. This ribbon went particularly well with my sister's radiant face and her big dark eyes that glittered with joy. To complement this outfit my sister wore a tan velvet hat with the brim turned up. And thus she went about all winter long—even when it was freezing outside. She used to wear her outfits in rotation, changing once a week; while she wore one, she mended the other.

My sister had many girlfriends and acquaintances. She also had her fair share of admirers among the teenage boys, who often called on her and with whom she took strolls down Bol'shaia Street. The young folks from the V. family were constant fixtures in our home. We and the V. family came from the same region. What's more, our grandparents lived in Bobruisk and our parents in Vil'na. The V. boys would come by to visit my sister. Perhaps they knew that Faitel' Paperna (by this time Father had reembraced his Jewish name) had a second daughter, but I never showed myself to anybody. The minute someone stopped by the house, I would hide behind the partition (in our new apartment, I would hide in my own room). When our sister Idochka got older, she had a governess—Klara Pavlovna, from Riga. Friends of my parents and sister were certain that Klara Pavlovna was, in fact, Faitel' Izrailovich's second daughter. Indeed, she played a most lively role in our family's affairs. I came out of the shadows only much later, when I had entered the Higher Women's Courses and stopped avoiding people.

My sister, a tenderhearted altruist, devoted all of her attention to me with every fiber of her being. She didn't take the place of my mother, but she was indeed a mother to me and loved me to the point of self-sacrifice, even after she married and had her own children. My brother-in-law was not jealous, because she had love enough for all those close to her, but there were times when he would frown upon the bonds between us. Children do not usually think too much about such things; they believed that this was how it was supposed to be, that everybody should love Aunt Andzia (as I was called at home).

In mentioning this, I want to jump forward just a bit and relate an episode that sheds light on my relationship with my sister. For their ten-year anniversary, my sister's husband gave her a diamond brooch. As soon as they saw it, both of my nieces, with one voice, cried out: "Mamochka, is this for Aunt Andzia?" They were used to everything pretty in the house being set aside for me. Of course, this was not to my brother-in-law's liking. I think that the reason for my sister's exceptional devotion was my weak constitution, my helplessness, and my naïveté. I must say that my sister repaid me a hundred times over for the absence of our mother's caresses. I think that our stepmother was not entirely comfortable with the relationship between us—perhaps this was what distanced me from her and my father.

I was very anemic during my gymnasium years, and I required a hearty diet, strolls in the fresh air, and so forth. My sister saw to all of these needs, but it was not easy for her to deal with me. When I agreed to go for a walk, I would do so on one condition—that we take Sirotskaia Street, so as not to run into anyone I knew. I was under doctor's orders to go skating, and I loved to go to the skating rink early in the morning before the crowds had started to gather. During our lunch break at school, my sister would bring me a fresh cutlet. We were not allowed to bring food from home onto school premises, so my sister arranged matters with the watchman so that I could eat my cutlet in his quarters. Usually, I could eat scarcely a third of a portion, and my sister would return home distressed and out of sorts.

At school, despite my physical weakness, I was what they call a sly one. I would sit there with an innocent look on my face and make my girlfriends laugh by cracking jokes at our teachers' expense. I never received an A for conduct. I especially loved making fun of the homeroom teachers, and I always found a biting little word for each of them. Of course, I had school friends during those years. But in this, too, I failed to please my parents. As the respectable Vil'na residents they were, my parents wanted me to make friends with young people from their circle, but, alas, one of my school friends came from a very poor family, and the other's father had a bad reputation.

I was talkative with my girlfriends: we chatted about what we read, what we were thinking, but often we just joked and laughed; this is perfectly natural in one's youth. In terms of what they knew about the world, both of my girlfriends were far more advanced than I.

At the age of sixteen or seventeen, affairs of the heart usually begin to play a big role in a girl's life. One of my two friends had already had considerable experience in that department. This astonished me. Her mother had given birth to more than twenty children. She was the youngest and the only one who was still alive, and so they'd given her several names (such was the superstition). Her face was not especially attractive; her eyes alone were pretty, blazing with some special sort of fire. Nowadays they would say that she had "sex appeal." She enjoyed great success, but on a certain occasion her luck ran out. In those days we had a real lady-killer in Vil'na, one that no girl could resist—all the girls fell in love with him, despite the fact that he was a hunchback. Try and figure out a woman's soul! When she met him for the first time in public, my girlfriend swore that she would not fall in love with him. Offended, the young man made her a proposition: "Let's make a wager. Give me two weeks, with the condition that we take a stroll every day for two hours, and you will fall in love with me!" She was so sure of herself that she thought nothing of agreeing to such a risky venture. They began their daily strolls the very next day, down by the railroad tracks. The topics of their conversations were primarily abstract: in those days, young people often struck up deep friendships on the basis of such conversations. Day by day, my girlfriend set off on these walks with greater interest and enthusiasm, and soon enough she was aquiver with anticipation for their meetings. At first she would share all her impressions with us, but she soon forgot all about her girlfriends. Meanwhile, the fourteenth day arrived and the young man, taking his leave, informed her that now their walks had come to an end. Not a single word more. He bowed politely and walked away. She was beside herself for a long time to come; she had fallen for him, head over heels, you see. This was her first powerful love, and thus a great blow to her pride. Time and youth, however, are the best healers. In the end, my girlfriend married a teacher who worked at the Jewish primary school and came from a small village and, following her mother's example, gave birth to a whole clutch of kids. I saw her only once thereafter—she had let herself go, grown flabby, and become a provincial "lady."

I'll say a few words, too, about my other girlfriend. She was a lively girl, kind, practical, straightforward, a girl who didn't aim too high. She was one of the best students in our gymnasium. The need for love and a healthy maternal instinct awakened early in her, and so, without thinking too long on it, she got married to the first man who set his sights on her. He was a young pharmacist, unremarkable in every way. It's bad to say, I know, but it seemed to me in those days a pharmacist was the very epitome of insularity and drabness. Many, many years later, after having gone to Petersburg in search of enlightenment, I happened to remember my old friend from long ago and went to call on her. I found her behind the counter at an apothecary's shop, wearing a wide cotton coat. She hadn't changed much at all: her face was as kind, welcoming, and merry as ever, though life had dealt her a hard hand. She had lots of kids, each one littler than the last, but in each of them she found some special qualities to cherish. Her husband had eye problems, and blindness threatened. The entire business was in her hands, and at the same time she managed to help her children with their homework. What a healthy, normal specimen! She showed little interest in me personally, however, and we never saw each other again.

<h1 style="text-align:center">VII</h1>

It is not easy for me to recount the period of my youth, not because I do not want to write or because I am ashamed. When I wrote about my childhood years, individual pictures presented themselves, etched firmly in my memory, but now I can't speak of pictures so much as the feelings—often unclear—of a young, innocent soul, as impressionable as a flower. It's almost impossible to convey the nuances of such feelings: even a great artist finds it hard to recall from memory his first song, inspired by a meeting with a beloved girl. Now I regret that I did not keep a notebook and that I did not save any letters. But in this realm—the realm of intimate feelings—I have always followed my own path.

Unlike my girlfriends, I did not care for intimate conversations. I truly suffered whenever one of my girlfriends happened to mention the name of a certain young man whom I found attractive. I felt myself blushing all over, and the more I tried to control myself, the more I lost my composure. Sometimes I would have liked to tell my girlfriends that a certain fellow had been at our house yesterday and that he and I had talked all evening long, but I refrained, knowing that I would give myself away by the mere mention of his name. This young man who was my first love was a schoolmate of my older brother and was often at our house. I understood that B.'s visits were a mere pretense for seeing and talking with me. As if by accident, I would drop by the study, where my brother did his homework, and if I should happen to see B., I would sometimes remain there for quite a while. He would sit there for hours at a time, without removing his military overcoat. B. came from a prominent bourgeois family who had distinguished themselves from others in the same set by their wicked ways. He himself was the exception in the family. He was tall in stature, with well-proportioned features and sorrowful eyes. He read a great deal, and thought a great deal, as well.

Around the same time, as it so happened, I also became acquainted with a classmate of B.'s named Sasha. He was also good-looking, but simpler and more natural: a kind and cheerful young man. I enjoyed spending time in their company—it was nice to be serious with one and joke around with the other. Sasha openly courted me, which troubled me a great deal. His face was kind, handsome, and good, and always seemed to say: "I'm prepared to go through hell and high water for you!" He was always doing nice things for me and looking out for me. He was very good with his hands, and once he crafted a beautiful and unique walking stick from a tree branch, coated it with lacquer, and engraved our initials on it. I used it for many years afterward, and in the summertime I loved to go down country paths with that walking stick. My friend also carved our initials on some benches in the secluded corner of the garden, and we often sat there in the evenings. The benches themselves have long since rotted away, but the carved letters are still there today, on the railing of the upper balcony of our house. Sasha protected me on our strolls, but he did not treat me as if I were made of glass; when we swung on the swing, he would push me so high that it simply took my breath away. It was scary and fun at the same time. I believed that if he were near me, then nothing bad could happen to me.

Sasha was a good dancer, and I loved to dance, too. I remember one time, when we were visiting my sister, someone sat at the piano and played, "A maiden went to fetch water, a young fellow went to fetch her . . ." I pulled out a kerchief, lifted it high over my head, placed my hands on my hips, and started dancing, kicking out my legs, slowly at first, and then faster and faster. My eyes blazed, my cheeks grew flushed, and my long, thick braid started to come undone. I felt so happy then: happy with the knowledge that I was loved, and that life was so beautiful and so interesting! Naturally, Sasha was pulled toward me like a compass needle to a magnet, and we started dancing. Everyone gathered round us in a circle and started clapping in time to the music and singing along, feasting their eyes on us. I felt my partner draw nearer to me, his hot breath touching me, the beating of his heart, his admiring gaze—and suddenly, I froze in place, as if startled by an excess of emotion. Everyone was at a loss—what had happened, why had I stopped dancing? I looked at Sasha—he stood there, confused and troubled. How sorry I felt for him, but my soul felt at ease. It's so nice to realize that you are dear to the person who is kind to you and close to you. I needed nothing more.

In those days, I spent the summers with my sister, at Pushkarnia, where she lived year-round—her husband was the director of a paper factory.[14] I remember the walks we used to take in Pushkarnia—me, my brother, and my two friends. I'm not ashamed to admit that I enjoyed their rivalry over me. Each tried to distinguish himself in my presence: one with his endless devotion, which he professed each step of the way; the other with his restraint and composure, which, it seems, impressed me more. During one of our strolls, it grew dark and cold on the walk home. My hands were stiff with cold, so B. took my hand and slipped it inside his pocket, warming my hand with his; we walked like this almost all the way back to town. As soon as I became aware of this, I realized that this must be the cause of much grief for my other devoted friend. This was sinful and cruel of me, but at the same time it was pleasant and enjoyable, even though I knew that I was doing wrong. All of these feelings—whether joyous or mournful—I kept to myself, never sharing them with my girlfriends.

Later, during my years at university, being a lover of music, I would often go to the Petersburg opera. While listening to *Evgenii Onegin,* I was attracted simultaneously to both Onegin and Lenskii.[15] The heroes of my first "romance" reminded me of these lovers. In my "romance" (I don't know whether this is really the right word for it), there were no kisses, no displays of passion: it was spun from the very finest feelings of a young, daydreaming soul. I decided to write about this because it seems to me that such feelings were typical for young girls of our day.

Affairs of the heart could not, however, make my life complete. I suffered from an emptiness within and was burdened by the situation around me. After completing my studies at the gymnasium, I had to spend three whole years sitting around the house with nothing to do, and I came to feel a strong dissatisfaction with myself and others. My parents were typical Jewish merchants, with a certain bent toward intellectual pursuits. Papasha, for example, read Tolstoy with great enthusiasm. At the same time, he studied Boborykin no less eagerly and managed to read his collected works in their entirety.[16] Mamasha considered herself a connoisseur of the German classics and loved to show off her literary knowledge. She was well-versed in the Talmud, as well. Their forays into the realm of literature were undertaken mostly on the Sabbath, after an afternoon nap and over a glass of tasty tea. I did not take part in these conversations. At home, among my family at the table, I kept silent, and this was quite uncomfortable for me. At times, though I wanted to say a few words to be polite, I could not manage to come up with anything, no matter how hard I tried. My tongue was tied, and nothing could untangle it. Everyone sat in a circle, conversing with much liveliness, but I felt out of sorts. Nothing they had to say was of interest to me.

My parents talked mostly about business, and this depressed me. After each meal I would go straightaway to my room, while the other members of the family remained in the dining room. I began to distance myself somewhat from my girlfriends, too. My spiritual dissatisfaction, my desire for a better life, the striving toward what is good, toward self-improvement—all this was alien to them. I felt myself alone. Fortunately, I possessed a certain persistence in striving to achieve my goals. I firmly resolved that I would not remain in my current condition for long. In those days, in certain circles of society, girls were being drawn toward higher education. By some sort of miracle, this wave reached me as well.

VIII

And so began the period of my longing for a new life, a life that would be responsive to my needs. No one close to me had any sympathy whatsoever for my plans, and it was no use imagining that anyone might render me any assistance. No one from Vil'na had ever gone to Petersburg to attend the Higher Women's Courses, and since I knew that my parents would never consent to my going to Petersburg, I formulated a plan that seemed to me easier to implement. It consisted of remaining in Vil'na, applying for the Women's Courses at Kiev, and then, in the spring, traveling there to take the first-year entrance examinations. Once I'd taken the exams, I could probably arrange it so that I would not have to return to Vil'na. Having made my decision, I sent a copy of my diploma to the Women's Courses. Moreover, I pawned all of my dead mother's jewelry so that I could reserve a place in the Courses. They sent me all the necessary books from Kiev, and I began to study in earnest. I enrolled in the department of history and philology. I still remember how I suffered through Old Church Slavonic grammar, which I mastered with great difficulty. Of everything that I worked so hard to learn, only one thing has stuck in my memory—the vocative case of *zhena* is *zheno*!

Spring came, and, with my heart pounding, I announced to my parents that I had decided to go to Kiev to enroll in the Women's Courses. I was still unsure of myself. As I've mentioned, our Mamasha was known for her mind and her eloquence. She phrased the question in completely different terms. "You're striving for an education," she said, "and I completely understand you. We're not going to deny you this because we begrudge you the money—on the contrary, we're ready to give you as much education as you need. You can study anything you want and take lessons from the best teachers in Vil'na, but stay home, don't disgrace our family. Look at other people—I don't know a single girl in Vil'na who would live alone in a strange city!" I had not anticipated Mamasha's line of argument, but I was unable to put aside my desire for a new and richer life, one that would nourish both my mind and my heart. And so I remained in Vil'na and began in earnest to study physics, chemistry, and Russian literature.

The chemist Polozov, the local inspector of the *Realschule* and a well-known educator, taught me chemistry and physics. It's amusing to recall how the two of us sat for hours on end in the makeshift "lecture hall" of his apartment (the children's bedroom)—he in the role of professor, delivering a two-hour lecture on the theory of chemistry, and I in the role of student. My homework was to write out in longhand everything that I had heard. My lessons in literature were carried out in the same spirit, although another lecturer taught them, of course.

Despite how serious I was in those days, I was not averse to having fun. Young ladies at the time did not go to balls by themselves; their parents brought them out "into society," as it were. I remember how I casually allowed myself to get talked into attending one such ball. A light blue wool dress was sewn for me (at that time only married women wore silk). The skirt was narrow and unpleated, with chiffon lace beneath; the bodice was close-fitting, with both sides draped in pleats, in the shape of a fan. The entire dress was set off with lace: little pink flowers were embroidered on the light blue tulle. A high collar fit snugly around the neck. The sleeves reached only to the elbows—this was the only whim I permitted myself, because I had long gloves. This was my very first ball. I was entering society from my own self-imposed seclusion. The music, the lighting, the dances, with "Onegin" and "Lenskii" there as well—all this made my head spin. It seemed to me at that moment that the whole world belonged to me, that I was the very center of the earth, and that no one in the world was happier than I.

I presented myself in society for the first time that night. Everyone looked at me with curiosity, and I saw that they liked me. In my ordinary, everyday life I not only did not seek to be admired but would sooner do everything possible to avoid people. There was a certain sort of duality in my nature, which caused me no small amount of grief. Remaining at home became more and more of a burden to me every day. I kept to myself more and more; I looked at people sullenly, from beneath furrowed brows, and grew more critical of everything around me. Everything that was said at the dinner table irritated me. I even gradually began to grow cool toward Uncle Grigorii, the only person with whom I shared my thoughts (by this time he had given up teaching and lived with his family in Vil'na). My parents, it seems, had stopped worrying about me. Mamasha, satisfied that she had fenced me in so cleverly, transferred all her worries to my sister.

As it turned out, Mamasha had her reasons for renting out our best room to her cousin. At eighteen, my sister considered herself fully grown, and my parents decided to marry her off to our new lodger. Mamasha's plan could not have come off better. The fiancé she'd chosen worked in a bank and was already self-sufficient. A young man like that needs a wife from a good family, a wife who's young and healthy and not without a dowry. Sister met these requirements completely, plus she was a good person and had a pleasant personality. Papasha was the only one, however, who felt that in all honesty Sister was not serious enough, that she was too frivolous and could not make a respectable man happy. He could never forgive my sister for having once remarked at the dinner table: "I don't want to live to an old age (that is, forty), I want to die young so that everyone will pity me and grieve that such a young girl died!" Papasha even considered it his duty to forewarn the fiancé not to be too hasty with a decision on which the fate of his entire future would hang. But fortunately the young seldom pay heed to the counsel of the old. All the talk at home centered around my sister's imminent betrothal. I was the only one who knew nothing of all this.

And so one fine evening there was a big affair. The tables were set, and we prepared for our guests to arrive. Uncle Grigorii stopped by my room to relate the joyous news that today was my sister's engagement party and that our lodger was to become her fiancé. As soon as I heard this I started to weep; for some reason I feared for my sister's well-being. I cried and cried, and then, washing my face, I got dressed again and went out to the dining room to take part in the celebrations. I loved my sister very much and could not imagine that this unattractive, uninteresting, and, it seemed, overly respectable fellow was the one with whom my beloved sister would be forever bound! Fortunately, my fears were unfounded. You can't measure someone else by your own standards, and my sister found happiness in her married life.

And yet my parents still were not satisfied. They were particularly unhappy that my admirer "Lenskii" continued to court me, and they feared I would marry him. Reflecting on this, it's funny to think how far off such thoughts were from me. I don't know why my parents disliked "Lenskii" so. He was the son of a local doctor. On the other hand, they had nothing against "Onegin"—he was the only son of a wealthy family. "Onegin's" parents, however, had long ago promised him in marriage to a wealthy relative whom they had raised in their home. In fact, they were very much afraid that he would be smitten with me and thus ruin their plans. In the summers, our parents would stay at their dachas in Bel'mont, on the outskirts of

Vil'na.[17] I remember how we would eagerly resume our friendship each summer. We would lie on the forest grass, but within twenty minutes my companion would be called home, either for tea or for lunch. This would always make me chuckle, but for him, I noticed, it was awkward. Truth be told, however, there was nothing to bind us together; we were completely different people.

IX

I could not abandon the thought of escaping from home. As time went on, it became clearer to me that life was about more than just receiving an education in physics or chemistry, that there was something more meaningful than everyday concerns, that "man does not live by bread alone!" Once again I began to think hard about how to escape from the mud that ensnared me. I even began to fear that this mud would somehow suck me in. I broke ties with all my old friends, without making any new ones. But this did not distress me; I'd grown accustomed to coming to grips with my own problems. I firmly believed that if your goal in life was clear, you could always find the path toward its realization; one has only to want it badly enough.

As strange as it may seem, I finally made the decision to enter the Higher Women's Courses in Petersburg during a serious illness, when everyone was worried for my life. The doctor who treated me had little faith that I would recover. I had dysentery and lay in bed six weeks. This was toward the end of the summer, when all the vacationers had already left the countryside and returned to Vil'na.

We were still in Pushkarnia, where my sister lived, and so she moved back in with us and tended to my needs day and night with her usual self-sacrifice. I became so weak and thin that it was hard to recognize me. I remember that I was given a tablespoon of castor oil three times a day, day in and day out. Of course, I behaved capriciously at the time. One day when I was especially nervous and refused to take the castor oil, my sister brought out two tablespoons of the stuff and, in an effort to lift my spirits, drank one straight down, while smacking her lips. This heroic act had its effect on me. I felt ashamed and drank my dose. While I was sick in bed, I carried on a lively correspondence with a girl from school who had lived in Petersburg and who also was preparing to enroll in the Women's Courses. In the end, my body prevailed over the illness, and my strength was gradually restored.

That autumn was marvelous, and the air was fresh and aromatic. I remember being able to see ripe, rosy apples and pears from my bedroom window. My sister and those friends who had not abandoned me chatted gaily among themselves at my bedside. I noticed that they would leave and come back one at a time, and, from their faces, I could see that they had treated themselves to a little something—it must have been a fruit freshly picked from the tree. I begged them not to think they had to hide such things from me—after all, I was a sensible person, and I understood that I was not yet allowed to eat fruit. But as soon as their teeth began to crunch into those juicy apples, large tears streamed down my face: my little experiment had failed, and it pained me, and I was full of shame.

Another week went by, and I was able to get out of bed for the first time. I experienced an unforgettable sensation: my body had become so light and weightless that I could not stand on my own two legs. I had to be supported on either side. My legs dangled about like those of a six-month-old baby who finds himself upright for the very first time and helplessly kicks about in a vain attempt to walk. But youth conquers all, and within a week we were able to move back to Vil'na. From that moment on, I began with feverish energy to make my preparations to enroll in the Women's Courses at Petersburg.

In addition to my gymnasium diploma, I also needed a certificate of political loyalty, a certificate stating that I had taught for the past two years, and, since I was a minor, written permission from my father. Obtaining each of these pieces of documentation caused me an enormous amount of worry, distress, and humiliation. My first concern was the certificate of political loyalty. In these matters, I had no experience whatsoever (nor do I even now). All at once I felt completely helpless, and so I let my elder brother in on my little secret. The petition was written and submitted to the governor's chancellery. From there it was forwarded to the police precinct, where they were supposed to conduct a thoroughgoing investigation into whether or not I was politically reliable.[18]

My trials and tribulations began from that moment forth. I went to the police precinct almost every day to check and see if my paperwork was completed, and invariably the officer would respond by shaking his head without even looking up at me. Some holiday or other was approaching, and I rejoiced that I wouldn't have to make a trip to the station. But the very next day, early in the morning, a notice arrived at my parents' store, summoning me to appear at the precinct. What I feared might happen had indeed come to pass.

You can imagine how anxious my parents were. They immediately called my older brother to the store and sent him to the precinct to ask why they had called me in. Naturally, my brother did not go to the precinct but went straight home and shared with me the joyous news. We discussed the situation and decided that he would tell our parents that I'd supposedly seen a fistfight while walking down Nemetskaia Street, and now I was being summoned to the precinct as a witness. When he returned to the store, my brother calmed our parents, and they were glad that all their worries had been for nothing.

X

The time was drawing near for me to enroll in the Women's Courses, and I grew impatient. Though he was ready to go through hell and high water for me, my brother was of little use, and so I turned to my sister. She had already matured into quite a sensible person and never lost her composure. When she found out that I had made up my mind to move to Petersburg, she was quite distressed but nevertheless devoted all her energies to helping me. And so it was that we set out for the precinct together. My sister's beauty made quite an impression on the officer. He inquired politely as to the nature of her business, and my sister whispered that she wanted to speak with him in private in his office.

He gallantly showed her the way, and I followed. My sister requested that my paperwork be expedited and immediately placed a three-ruble note on the table. This gesture produced a magical effect. Straightaway the officer declared: "Don't worry about a thing, go home. Tomorrow morning you will receive your certificate at the governor's chancellery." I couldn't see myself in a mirror, but I must have had a look of utter astonishment on my face. Here I was so exhausted, and the solution had been quite simple all along!

Then began all the rigmarole to obtain certification that I had taught. The problem was that our gymnasium did not have an eighth grade, so I had to receive written documentation from two families saying that I had taught their children. On the basis of this written documentation, the public school inspector could issue me the certificate. I submitted the appropriate petition. A few days later, when I once again appeared at the chancellery to pick up the certificate, the inspector himself walked out and began to swear and yell at me. His short, thick neck grew so red that I was afraid he would have a stroke right then and there. Finally, he stormed back into his office and returned with my petition in hand. Striking the paper with his fist, he yelled at me in a high, strange voice that bore little resemblance to his normal one: "Just what do you think the directory of public schools is, anyway? You think this is some kind of garbage dump we're running here?"

By the time he was done shouting, it seemed that he too was frightened that his heart might give out, and so he proceeded to lower his voice two octaves. It was at that point that I realized my blunder: as it happened, I had forgotten in my petition to address the inspector by his proper title, "Your Excellency." I was informed that it would take at least a month to receive my certificate.

The next day I wrote a new petition in which I addressed the inspector as "Your Most High Excellency" and repeated the title a number of times throughout. I stopped by the office regularly, hoping that I would receive a response. Each time, the civil servants who worked in the chancellery would reply that, unfortunately, the inspector would not budge. After two weeks had passed, a clerk came up to me and whispered: "He's just come back from a hearty breakfast and is in a good mood. When he steps out of his office to meet the petitioners, walk right up to him, and I'll hand him your petition to sign on the spot."

And thus it was that I received both of the documents I needed. After all this, it seemed that obtaining my father's permission would be a simple matter. The encounter with the police officer and the inspector might have been frightening, but I did not think that Father would be so difficult to convince. Papasha was a gentle,

weak-willed person; it was Mamasha who played the leading role
in our household, in financial and familial matters alike. I do not
think that, in her heart, she was against me, but she felt uneasy
all the same. All the other mothers from the so-called educated
set flew into a tizzy and warned Mamasha not to let me go or else
their daughters would follow my example and fly out from under
their own mothers' wings. As it so happened, only two other
girls from Vil'na went to the Courses, and neither one belonged
to our "upper set." Mamasha, though, did not relish the prospect
of being practically the first mother in her social circle (and a
stepmother, no less) to let her daughter set out for a "foreign land"
like Petersburg. At my parents' request, Uncle Grigorii discussed
the matter with me quite often, in an effort to change my mind.
But this only lowered his standing in my eyes. I did not debate
with him but listened to him patiently and respectfully. It took all
the strength I could muster, but I remained steadfast. I understood
my uncle's position, and I took no offense.

Convinced that my decision was final and that this time I would
not give in, my sister discussed my plans over and over again with
my parents, pleaded with them, begged, and wept. On more than one
occasion, with tears in her eyes, she tried to persuade me to remain
in Vil'na, but I held my ground.

XI

We spent the next two months in a very tense atmosphere. The
supreme family council, chaired by Mamasha, resolved to press
forward by other means, in the hopes that all might yet work out
for the best! And so it was that one day, while I was sitting in my
room, I heard a strange voice coming from the dining room, where
the family was gathered round the table. Right then and there, of
course, I decided not to come out to the dining room.

Uncle Grigorii came by and tried convincing me, in most
ingratiating tones, to come out to the dining room for an hour or
so. "A very handsome young man is sitting here," he said, "and your
parents hope that you might take a liking to him—this would be

a brilliant match." I was taken aback; my parents must not really understand me at all if they thought they could present me with such an offer!

But my uncle was persistent. "No one is forcing you," he said. "Go out and meet him, and then decide for yourself." I managed to regain my composure. "Fine, I'll go out there," I told him, "but I doubt my parents will be pleased with me." My sister asked me to change my clothes, but I did not bother, and with a heavy heart I stepped out into the dining room. I sat there at the table like a deaf mute, not looking up at anyone. After tea, everyone retired to the study, and the two of us found ourselves alone. I replied tersely and sharply to each one of our guest's questions.

"What are you doing these days?" he asked. "Probably studying foreign languages?"

"I don't even think of such things—that may be fine for young ladies looking to get married, but I have no such desires, and, in general, I find it a useless waste of time; one can be an educated person without knowing foreign languages . . ."

Our conversation proceeded in this spirit for a little while, and then I fell completely silent. They must have been watching us, and, finally, my uncle came in and sat down beside the unlucky suitor. I took advantage of this opportunity and returned to my room. This was the first and last time, it seems, our prospective suitor paid us a visit. I didn't discuss any of this with my uncle, my sister, or my parents—all the more so because I knew that an explanation would not amount to much, and besides, explaining myself is not in my nature.

Now, as I describe how I used to behave at home, I recall a certain episode from my days as a schoolteacher. I used to enjoy having conversations with the children over breakfast on various topics. Once I posed to them a question: "Tell me, with your hand on your heart, do you behave yourself at home as well as you do at school?" One of the schoolchildren, nine-year-old Vitya, blushing bright red, replied: "To tell you the honest truth, Anna Pavlovna, at home I'm unbearable!" I might well echo his confession—at home I too was unbearable. My family was offended by the way I conducted myself. They knew that I could be cordial, cheerful, and talkative when I wanted to be.

XII

Amid these busy, anxious times, Uncle Avraam's oldest son happened to be passing through Vil'na. From a very early age, Gorats (as we called him in the family) distinguished himself by his remarkable abilities. Already at the age of seven he was a specialist in ancient and medieval history, and at eight he entered the fourth class. Although we had had little in common back in Plotsk (at the time I was yet a small baby), in Vil'na we met as equals. He stayed with us for only two days, but the encounter made a strong impression on me. At the time my cousin was already a student in the Faculty of Natural Sciences at St. Petersburg University. He possessed such vast and varied knowledge, and he was so well read, that I must confess I was afraid to bring up frivolous topics in conversation with him.

He sympathized with my desire to break loose from home and promised to help me. There was nothing remarkable about my cousin's appearance: he was not very tall; he had long, fair hair and a reddish beard; his face was covered with tiny pimples; his eyes were clear and always seemed focused on something far off in the distance. His voice was melodious, of a pleasant timbre, and sincere. Most of all, one noticed his extraordinary modesty and his tendency toward self-effacement, to cede center stage to others. Like most students of the day, he dressed shabbily: a frayed, worn-out suit; a plain Russian peasant shirt beneath the jacket; and on top of it all, a threadbare overcoat, which saw service in winter and summer alike. In the wintertime he wore a kerchief round his neck. It was thick and heavy, like the kind a cook wears, but it provided little warmth. In those days, wearing such an article was a sign of one's ideological convictions.

After talking with our guest to my heart's content, I suggested that we take a walk so that we might have a look at the beautiful countryside. He asked me: "Wouldn't it make you uncomfortable, walking around with me on the street?" I became indignant—striking up a friendship with such a thoughtful and serious young man made me feel better about myself. What foolish notions came into his head!

Two days flew by, as if in a dream, and then my cousin left, having promised to make inquiries around Petersburg and to write often. After his departure, however, I did not receive a single letter. This surprised me very much, since he had taken such an interest in me!

Later on, when I found myself in Petersburg, he explained that he had written many times and had once even sent a telegram, but his letters were never passed on to me. It seems my parents kept a sharp lookout for my cousin's correspondence and immediately destroyed his letters. For some reason they were convinced that it was Gorats who was to blame for my stubbornness in wanting to leave home.

At last the time for my departure drew near. Some time ago I had filled out the paperwork that Papasha needed to sign and placed it on his desk in an envelope. Every day, for two months, I would check the desk anxiously, in search of Father's signature. When they saw how inflexible I was, my uncle and my sister persuaded Papasha to sign the paper. Father, however, was in no hurry, hoping to drag things out and weaken my resolve.

One morning my sister noticed me bustling about my dresser—taking out clothes, a few blouses, and some books, and packing everything in a suitcase. In a frightened voice she asked: "What are you doing?"

"I am leaving today," I answered calmly. It was nine o'clock in the morning, and the train was scheduled to depart at eleven! Sister left the room and came back a few minutes later with our parents. Tears began to flow, as if it were my funeral! Sister wept uncontrollably. The cook dropped what she was doing, ran in from the kitchen, and started bawling. Basia, our poor relation, took advantage of the opportunity to shed a few tears for her own bitter orphan's lot in life. Papasha tried to get me to promise that I would be gone for only a year. I replied that I was leaving with the firm resolve to spend four years at the Women's Courses, until I had graduated.

Papasha did not sign the papers, but all the same he gave me enough money for the trip, and thirty rubles for the first month. I gave Papasha and Mamasha a rather perfunctory kiss, clasped Basia's hand warmly (at the time, my brothers were away at the gymnasium), and left the family nest.

My sister escorted me to the train station. There we hugged each other tightly, and she sobbed ever so loudly. I took my seat on the train, without any emotion whatsoever. In the most serious moments of my life, I've never been able to cry, even though tears make it easier to cope.

And so, finally, I set off into the wide world, a world that was unknown to me, but so alluring!

CHAPTER THREE

Student Years

(St. Petersburg, 1885–89)

I

Vil'na—with its short and narrow streets, where the street names
changed every few blocks and the infamous cobblestone causeways
bruised the feet of horses and people alike. From Vil'na, I found myself
in the capital with its imposing downtown thoroughfare, Nevskii
Prospekt, stretching from the Moscow Station all the way to the
Admiralty. Nevskii Prospekt is remarkable for its breadth, not only
compared to the streets of Vil'na, but even when measured against
the standard of other European capitals. The road is paved with layers
of eight-sided wooden blocks. Up and down its entire length there
are restaurants, coffeehouses, stores with luxurious window displays,
with all sorts of exotic plants and enticing delicacies.

The sights of Nevskii Prospekt produce an immediate and powerful
impression. Buildings with splendid entryways and porters dressed
in livery; the Kazan Cathedral with its columns that resemble those
of St. Peter's Basilica in Rome; the shops at Gostinyi Dvor, whose
stalls seem ready to burst from an abundance of expensive goods; the
magnificent massiveness of the Winter Palace; the splendid granite
embankment; and the bridges scattered here and there across the
Neva River, all aglitter in the evenings with their numerous lights.
Richly appointed carriages race up and down the bridges, harnessed
to pairs of handsome chestnut bays or Tambov trotters, black as
ravens' wings. Perched atop the coach boxes sit drivers with broad
backs, soft thick beards, and a good-natured air of superiority about

them. A hired cab hitched to a trotter darts out, straining to pull a merchant crammed into the narrow seat, his jacket unbuttoned, outstretched legs stuffed into stylish pleated boots.

The typical Petersburg crowd is quite a curious one. At certain hours of the day the sidewalks are filled with office workers and urban dandies dressed neat as a pin in top hats, and with cold, flinty expressions on their faces to match the harsh and uninviting local climate; glittering young men sporting monocles in their right eyes; neatly groomed young ladies, plump and well-fed, who stroll about decorously in the company of their governesses. These types would promenade up and down Nevskii Prospekt, turning down Bol'shaia Morskaia Street. English, French, and German could be heard here more frequently than Russian. Among these well-dressed crowds, impoverished students could be spied, scurrying to the nearby Public Library, and female students, too, with bundles of books tucked under their arms.

In Petersburg, there were three modes of transportation available to mere mortals: seedy carriages for hire, horse-drawn trams that we "rich" students often used (five kopecks one way), and the incredibly clunky and uncomfortable omnibuses, nicknamed "the forty martyrs."[1] These last were used most commonly by lower-class women in shabby coats, down on their luck.

Petersburg makes a certain impression on a person coming from the countryside. I remember when my housekeeper's aged mother, who had lived her entire life in the village, came to visit. When she entered the kitchen, she clasped her hands and exclaimed: "The earth is so damp here, it's a wonder the buildings don't come tumbling down!"

When I first arrived in Petersburg, I stayed with Roza, a friend from the gymnasium, with whom I had kept up a correspondence. She lived with her sister on the square near the Aleksandrovskii Theater, across from the Public Library. Her sister had a big family of seven children, and an apartment fit for a nobleman. The head of the household was engaged in some important line of work. I spent about a week in that noisy house, where every evening at least seventeen people sat down at the dinner table.

On the day of my arrival, Roza and I set off to call on my cousin Gorats, who lived on the Petersburg Side of the city.[2] We took a horse-drawn tram, but once on the Petersburg Side we were obliged to wander down dark streets dimly lit by kerosene lamps. There were neither paved streets nor sidewalks in the neighborhood where Gorats lived. With some difficulty we were able to find his apartment in a courtyard with a number of wooden outbuildings. It turned out that Gorats lived in the most dilapidated building of them all.

We clambered up the steep wooden staircase and opened the tiny door. The air inside was so hot and humid it felt like a steam bath. The landlady, who lived in the kitchen, worked as a laundress and rented out two tiny rooms. Gorats occupied one of these rooms. He paid a mere pittance for the room, which was furnished in the typical student style: an iron cot with a small pillow and a thin, unquilted blanket; a large, unpainted table stacked high with books; two rickety chairs; and a washstand with a basin. It's funny that my cousin lived in such conditions for so many years and always ended up with landladies who were laundresses.

It came out in the course of our conversation that Gorats had written me often but that his letters had never reached me. When I informed him that I had still not received permission from my father to enroll in the Courses, this impractical young man responded with an invaluable piece of advice: no permission was needed to enroll in midwifery courses, and furthermore these courses gave one residency rights in the city. At Gorats's advice I wrote home that if I did not receive Father's permission immediately, I would enroll in the midwifery courses. My threat worked—my parents were frightened. It was bad enough that their daughter had left home to study, now she was planning to become a midwife. And so it was that the paperwork was sent.

II

It was with fear and excitement that I visited the Courses for the very first time. For three years I had dreamed that I would end up here, and now, finally, my dream had been fulfilled. The reality did not disappoint. On the contrary, I experienced a surge of energy, courage, and a belief in my own strength, a desire to be a part of this youthful, robust, meaningful, and interesting life. The courses were called the Bestuzhev Courses, after their founder, Bestuzhev-Riumin.[3]

The Courses had been in existence for about ten years before I arrived. In Russia there were always many donors for all sorts of causes, particularly for educational ones. Despite the somber mood that had settled in under the reign of Alexander III, the universities flourished. A Russian university education was of the highest quality, not only in the capitals, but in the other big cities of the empire as well. For women, however, there existed separate institutions of higher learning.

At first, the Courses were housed in a private apartment—on Gagarinskaia Street, I think. When I arrived in Petersburg, I found the Courses housed in a spacious, nicely equipped three-story building, located on the 10th Line of Vasil'evskii Island.[4] The building itself was splendid: lots of light and fresh air; wide, well-lit corridors; large common halls for recreation. The first floor housed the cloakroom, the cafeteria and kitchen, and the reading room. The two main lecture halls were built like amphitheaters and could accommodate up to five hundred students; the other lecture halls were smaller. The chemistry laboratory was equipped with the latest technological advancements: gas burners, hot and cold running water, cabinets to store chemicals and gases, and, moreover, a separate room for specialized work with hydrogen sulfide and so forth. Our laboratory at the Courses was considered better than the university's. We had physics labs with every possible instrument and spaces for tutorials with teaching assistants. The physiology labs, botany labs, and mineralogy labs were excellently equipped as well.

I started classes a month late, and by the time I arrived the Courses were teeming with people—all young girls, attractive, sincere, and serious. I simply sobbed with joy. That year there was an especially large influx of students, and my classmates, the first-year students, made the most noise of all, of course. As I was walking through the recreation hall, I heard a loud voice behind me: "Paperna, how did you wind up here? I never imagined that you would leave home to study!" As it turned out, this was T., one of the girls from my hometown who had also been admitted to the Courses. I had not been acquainted with her in Vil'na. T.'s father worked as a bookkeeper at the Jewish publishing house Romm (an old publishing firm that celebrated its one-hundred-year anniversary during my lifetime). T. struck me right away as an energetic and sensible girl, mature beyond her years.

These types of people stand out from the crowd and usually emerge as leaders. Afterward, I came to admire her a great deal and regarded her much more highly than I did myself.

I did not look like a real student—my "undemocratic" appearance hindered me, even though I dressed and wore my hair very modestly. I favored skirts and blouses and wore my hair in thick braids. The only thing that I fussed over was whether my hair covered my ears. To tell the truth, this was my way of striking a coquettish pose. I always wore very fine blouses. Since it was impossible to know all the students by name (there were more than three hundred first-year students in the Physics and Mathematics Faculty), I was known as the girl who always wore the fine blouses.

Our Courses were divided into three faculties: Natural Sciences, History-Philology, and Mathematics. I had long since made my decision as to which faculty I would enroll in. Like the majority of female students, I enrolled in Natural Sciences—such was the general mood of the times. The Bestuzhev Courses were regarded as the one true liberal oasis in those reactionary times and attracted all liberal-minded professors who were sympathetic to the cause of women's education. In no other European country at the time did so many women aspire to educate themselves as in Russia. The desire of female students in those days to strive for pure knowledge, combined with their desire to do good for the common people (such as the "going to the people" movement)—these were like rays of light penetrating the dark and dreariness of Russian life.[5]

III

The Higher Women's Courses had such famous lecturers as the chemist Mendeleev[6] and the physiologist Sechenov.[7] Incidentally, Sechenov and his wife, Vera Pavlovna, were the prototypes for the heroes in Chernyshevskii's novel, *What Is to Be Done?*[8] Other popular lecturers included Vagner, a zoologist and author of the charming *Fairy Tales for Grown-Ups*, which he wrote under the pen name of "Kitty Cat";[9] Borodin, a botanist and author of the fascinating book *Fertilization in the Vegetable Kingdom;*[10] the geologist Inostrantsev, thanks to whom new springs were discovered, including those at

Druskienniki, a health spa in Poland;[11] and Butlerov, a professor of inorganic chemistry who was renowned as an outstanding lecturer.[12] Besides the courses offered in our department, I also attended lectures in Russian literature by Orest Fedorovich Miller[13] (a well-known literary critic of the day) and Professor Kareev's[14] history lectures. During my first weeks at the Courses I felt like the happiest woman in the world. Every lecture seemed to me a magnificent revelation, and I drank in every idea, every word.

The physicist Borgman enjoyed great popularity as a lecturer, even though his experiments seldom went off as planned.[15] Each failed experiment concluded with the same remark to his assistant: "Well, Ivan Ivanych, it seems we forgot to prepare something or other." Whereupon he would turn to the students in the auditorium: "Pardon me, but it seems our efforts were unsuccessful." We always forgave him for these failures, since the lectures themselves were so interesting. He had, however, the bad habit of inserting "uh" into his lectures. On one occasion, the girl sitting next to me and I decided to count how many times he would say "uh" in the course of an hour. It so happened that we wasted a good fifteen minutes on this rather unproductive work. In spite of all this, when we found out that Professor Borgman intended to leave the Courses and teach only at St. Petersburg University, an entire delegation of students (myself included) came to him and pleaded with him to lecture at least half-time to us.

Besides Borgman, we also had another physicist on the faculty, Professor Gezekhus.[16] Although he was a more accomplished scientist than Borgman, his lecture hall was always empty, while Borgman's was packed. In the end, a group of students organized to make sure that at least a dozen or so students showed up to Gezekhus's lectures, so that he would not have to stand in front of an empty auditorium. In addition to scholarly expertise, a professor also has to possess a certain personal charisma to attract students.

I will not, of course, tell about each of our professors in detail, but I must say something about Professor Mendeleev's first lecture, which caused such a sensation among us. Mendeleev suggested to Nadezhda Vasil'evna Stasova[17] (who was the director of studies and the heart and soul of our Courses) that he might present to us a series of lectures concerning his remarkable discovery, the periodic table.

I remember the first lecture. It was held, of course, in the largest auditorium, which could seat about five hundred people, but more than twice that number turned out to hear Mendeleev. People sat on window ledges, on the steps, on the floor, beside the open doors, and even in the hall outside. Finally, squeezing through the crowd, Mendeleev himself strode in. He was tall, a bit stooped of shoulder, and carelessly dressed. He had a large head, long stringy hair that flew about in all directions, and eyes that always seemed to be staring off into the distance. A chart of his periodic table hung on the board behind him, and as he spoke all the elements in the table came alive, as if under the spell of his magic wand. It became clear why each element stood so firmly and inexorably in its rightful place and what sort of chemical affinity it shared with its closest neighbors. The empty spots between the elements began to speak as well, foretelling that at some future point they too would be filled in. The lecture lasted two hours, without a break, and the entire auditorium, students and professors alike, listened in rapt silence. After the lecture, the young crowd gave Mendeleev a huge ovation.

I cannot help but recall a particular anecdote that sums up Mendeleev's attitude toward his appearance. Once Mendeleev showed up for one of his lectures wearing an evening dress coat with tails. It was well made, of black woolen cloth, but it hung on the professor like a sack of potatoes. Beneath the black coat he wore a brown, double-breasted vest from an old, faded suit, and light-colored trousers with a narrow, brown leather belt; a bright shirt peeked out from between his vest and trousers; and around his neck, a soft collar with a black, crumpled necktie that hung off to one side. As I found out later, Mendeleev was decked out in this "dressy" attire because after the lecture he was scheduled to present a report to one of the government ministers.

I remember yet another occasion that showed Mendeleev as an extraordinarily brave and decisive man, ready to risk his own life in the name of science. In 1887 there was a solar eclipse, and Mendeleev decided to go up in a hot-air balloon to observe the phenomenon and record his observations. All the preparations had been made, but a thick fog had coated the outer casing of the balloon with condensation, rendering it impossible for two individuals to undertake the expedition. Mendeleev had intended to take off with a specialist who would steer the hot-air balloon, but now he asked the specialist to teach him how to operate the balloon himself. Time was of the essence, and so the specialist gave Mendeleev all the necessary instructions in the course of five minutes. Mendeleev himself went up in the hot-air balloon, carried out his observations, and safely landed in Klin, about eighty versts from Moscow.

And now I come to a certain incident concerning Professor Borodin. Almost all the students from our Courses attended his lectures. During one of these lectures, the professor was speaking about mushrooms. As he was listing each species of mushroom, he happened to remark in passing: "*Zhidy* don't eat this type of mushroom!" Silence always reigned during Borodin's lectures, but when he uttered the word *zhid*, the silence turned very grim indeed. No more than a minute or two passed before the entire lecture hall cleared out. Every one of the students made a point to walk out, and the professor was left there all alone. A delegation of students came to see him straightaway in his office, demanding that he apologize. He agreed at once. We all returned to the lecture hall, and the professor declared that the offensive word had slipped out accidentally. The incident was never mentioned again and was swiftly forgotten.[18]

Relations between professors and students at the Courses were excellent. The students respected the professors, and the professors maintained friendly relations with the students. I especially remember the merry student parties at the Courses, which professors too attended. Once we witnessed our very own Nadezhda Vasil'evna cutting the rug with Professor Sechenov, much to everyone's delight. We held Sechenov in particularly high esteem and regarded him as a wonderful man. And Nadezhda Stasova (the sister of the famous artist and critic) was also very much respected and valued by us. I'll say a few words about her later in connection with the story of a fellow student who was arrested right at the very height of the exam period.

For my part, I was filled with enthusiasm and placed my professors on a pedestal, as it were. But, it seems to me, they deserved it. In my four years at the Courses I was never disappointed. Our teaching assistants—future scholars themselves—were all exceptionally likable people as well. During my time in the Courses, we had two teaching assistants. One worked in the physics laboratory; the other was in the mathematics faculty.

In conclusion, I can say that the atmosphere at the Courses was wonderful. Our young people were infused with a mood of radicalism. Many of them took part in the nascent revolutionary movement, frequented revolutionary circles, took part in demonstrations, and were subjected to various disciplinary measures. Our Nadezhda Vasil'evna was forever bustling about to secure the return of *kursistki* who had been expelled.

IV

We students lived very modestly. I received thirty rubles each month from home to cover all of my expenses—room, board, books, transportation, and so forth—and I considered myself a wealthy student. Many of us lived on fifteen or even ten rubles a month.[19] They managed it thusly: five rubles for a double room, or two and a half rubles per person; lunch at the Courses (the cafeteria was managed by the students themselves) consisted of soup with boiled meat for ten kopecks, or soup without meat for five kopecks; bread was handed out for free, and in unlimited quantities. Of course, students on a budget did not very often get the soup with meat. Breakfast and dinner usually consisted of tea with a *kalach*. It never occurred to me to purchase something to go with the kalach.[20]

We did not use textbooks in our courses, but rather printed copies of lecture notes. Only the more well-to-do students purchased these notes; the other students simply borrowed them from their more privileged colleagues. The poorer students never attended the theater and hardly ever went ice skating. There were few wealthy students among us, but one who stood out was a certain Sibiriakova, whose family owned some very rich gold mines in Siberia. She donated a great deal of money to the Courses, and there were many students who received stipends thanks to her generosity. To look at her, she appeared no different from the other students and wore modest skirts and blouses. She cultivated a most egalitarian appearance.

I'll now say a few words about how I settled into life in Petersburg. At first, I had no luck finding a room. After staying with Roza's family for about a week, though, I decided that it was time for me to find my own place, someplace suitable for a student. Roza and I decided that we would room together, and we searched diligently for something close to Roza's sister's apartment, where we ate supper. We were determined to live like students—in other words, to live poorly and uncomfortably and without complaining about our fate. We wandered about the city for a long time before we found a place.

The room itself turned out to be rather uncomfortable and not exactly clean. The landlady lived with her so-called daughter, who apparently didn't have a job. The landlady was a great lover of animals, particularly those which gave off peculiar odors. She kept a regular menagerie, with rabbits, cats, dogs, even a hedgehog and a couple of hares, if I'm not mistaken. Not surprisingly, hardly anyone had shown any interest in the room, and this is probably why she was so eager to rent to us. But a few weeks later at Roza's sister's house, over supper, we happened to let slip that we had found a place on Meshchanskaia Street. A sudden look of astonishment came over Roza's brother-in-law, the color drained from her sister's face, and we realized that we had been found out. They demanded that we move out of there at once, because Meshchanskaia Street was considered indecent.[21]

I was puzzled as to why this was the case, but I did not want to press the matter. As soon as we returned home, we told the landlady that we did not like living on Meshchanskaia Street. The landlady was not at all surprised and suggested that she take a new apartment elsewhere in the city. She soon found an apartment on the Fontanka Canal, and we all moved in there. The landlady, naturally, brought her entire menagerie with her. But within two weeks, our peace and quiet came to an end. Though the afternoons were quiet, calm, and orderly, nighttime brought all sorts of loud noise, the crash of broken dishes, and drunken voices from the adjoining rooms. We couldn't figure out what the matter was, but the police swiftly stepped in and issued orders for our landlady to vacate the apartment within twenty-four hours. It seems that the sort of behavior permitted on Meshchanskaia Street was forbidden on the Fontanka. Once again, we had to find a new place to live. This time we took a decent room from a quiet family. And there we lived a normal, hardworking student life.

V

I usually spent the first half of the day at the Courses, listening to lectures or working in the laboratories (already during my first year). The remaining hours I spent in my room, reading books or, more often, journals. In those days, the thick monthly volumes touched on all sorts of social and scientific questions; some also gave monthly overviews of political events. Newspapers then did not possess the same significance that they do today. Journals played a vital role in young people's lives, and in their pages we searched for answers to all the questions that troubled and concerned our minds. Back then, there was much in the journals that had to be read "between the lines," as it were, and this made reading them all the more interesting. The Courses subscribed to nearly every periodical in print, and in multiple copies, too, so that we were always up to date with what was being published. One of the journals published Saltykov-Shchedrin's "Tales" in serial form. We all knew the exact date when the new issue would arrive, and already by morning a long line would form, each of us hoping to be the first to read the latest installment of Saltykov-Shchedrin. I remember that I especially liked the stories "Lost Conscience" and "The Carp Idealist."[22]

No sooner had I begun to grow accustomed to my studies and to make a few friends when the winter recess suddenly arrived—an entire month of vacation. In later years I went home for vacation, but this time no one invited me, and I really did not want to leave Petersburg. I sensed that my family still nursed a grudge against me, and I felt nothing tugging me back to that environment from which I had extricated myself with such difficulty. Besides, Petersburg is especially beautiful in the winter. It's marvelous to ride in a sleigh over the wide thoroughfares, and there's more sunshine in winter than in the autumn. Passersby are wrapped up in their fur coats, and the cabdrivers clap their gloves together merrily—the passengers are more generous in the wintertime. Though I had but little extra money, I felt happier than any one of them in their fine fur coats. I was young and in good spirits, and everything around me seemed new, interesting, and exciting.

After the winter recess, I began thinking about the upcoming examinations in the spring. We prepared for them both in the classroom and at home. It was then that I first noticed the great deficits in our learning and how ill prepared we Vil'na students were for university studies. We could not bring ourselves to ask one of our fellow students to help us with algebra and arithmetic, and so we took out an advertisement in the newspaper. A rather taciturn young Polish student answered our ad, and with his help we set about to fill in the blank spots in our mathematical knowledge. One girlfriend of mine, who hated mathematics, would sit there fuming during the lessons; she especially disliked math problems involving hypothetical cranes and pulleys of various heights. She hardly listened at all to our tutor's explanations, and so the bulk of the burden fell to me. I just felt so awkward around him!

We maintained very odd relations with our tutor. He gave us lessons until the spring holiday, and throughout that entire time we never exchanged a single word of small talk. By then, my girlfriend and I had become acquainted with two other students, the R. brothers, who also came from Vil'na and with whom we later became quite good friends. The brothers took turns tutoring us. When we failed to understand something, the older brother would flash an ironic smile, while the younger brother, who was a much more demonstrative sort, would fly into a rage and shout at us, flailing his arms about: "What do you mean you don't understand this? It's so simple!" Our mathematical skills did not improve one bit as a result of our lessons, but this was of little consequence to us. Truth be told, the lessons were not entirely unproductive: my girlfriend eventually married the older brother. I think he was charmed more by her beautiful, blue, mermaid eyes than her intellectual abilities.

I always used to feel quite stressed before exams. It was not that I had a fear of failing. During exams I was able to work with great focus, even taking pleasure in the excitement of the moment. What worried me, though, was that I felt uncomfortable standing before my professors armed only with such paltry knowledge—this was such a blow to my pride. It turned out that throughout the course of my future education—at the Teacher's Seminary in London, the Montessori Courses in Rome, and the Psychotechnical Courses in Paris—I never got through my examinations, and that is why I never received my diplomas, which, however, never really hindered my teaching. To this day, I am a great opponent of any sort of examination.

Because of my shy, retiring nature, I made few friends. Roza did not possess great social skills either. We socialized with other students only at the Courses—during lectures, in the laboratory, and in the study halls. I remember Antokol'skaia, who worked beside me in the laboratory and later became a prominent figure in the Society for the Promotion of Enlightenment among Jews.[23] I also became close with another student, Sleptsova—the daughter of the governor of Tambov province, who was later arrested during final exams— though we spent little time together. Among the male students who would visit us were the R. brothers, whom I have already mentioned, and my cousin Gorats. The R. brothers called on us quite often, and we would carry on lively conversations on the most diverse topics. Like Roza and me, the R. brothers frequented the opera, and we would share with one another our impressions, reminiscing about the most marvelous arias and the splendid acting.

VI

Gorats's visits were of a very different character. Gorats was a man of a particular stamp—a thinker, a philosopher. He was the very soul of all the scientific, philosophical, and literary reading circles of the day. After long debates he was always given the last word, and the young people would listen to his remarks with particular attention and respect. This respect was well deserved, since few people were such deep thinkers and few lived as true to their ideals as he. On account of his intense mental work, he experienced periods of stress and exhaustion. Gorats, however, was not a man of this world, and in everyday matters he was as helpless as a child. Once I received a postcard from him— without any salutation; written in his tiny, beadlike handwriting, it consisted of all of two lines: "If you don't purchase two colored shirts for me, I shall have to hang myself. Gorats."

He used to post a note on the door to his rooms asking his fellow students not to disturb him with their visits. It seems that my girlfriend and I were his only female acquaintances. He would call on us in order to help "cultivate" our personalities.

We were not particularly keen on reading books of philosophy, and so Gorats tried to expound for us, in popularized form, the theories of Kant and other thinkers. Although we ourselves never became philosophers, we nonetheless, thanks to our mentor, conscientiously pored over Darwin's *The Origin of Species*. To make sure that we were doing our reading, Gorats would visit us sometimes at eleven o'clock at night or even at six o'clock in the morning; his classes at the university began around eight in the morning.

He also took us to all sorts of reading groups and circles, including some illegal, underground ones. Among his acquaintances were a young couple who lived on the outskirts of Petersburg and were involved with preparing young people to conduct revolutionary propaganda. We were not initiated into this particular line of work, but on more than one occasion our room served as a warehouse for storing revolutionary literature. Once a large package arrived on our doorstep; it was heavy, likely containing some sort of weapons, and remained at our flat for about two months until the time came for summer vacation and we started packing our things to go home. Finally, through lengthy discussions involving persons unknown to us, it was decided to move the package to another location. The plan was as follows: I was to take the parcel and walk down a certain street on Vasil'evskii Island, where a student whose face I would recognize would be waiting for me. We had to slip through the gates very carefully—first he, and then I. This is how it all transpired. The student who was waiting for me wore a long overcoat; he took the package from me and slipped it under his coat, and then we parted ways, each going off in different directions. There was another package kept in our rooms, which we burned, on instructions from the persons who had brought it to us. Burning a package, however, is easier said than done, as anyone who has had to do it will tell you. Paper burns very slowly, and the strain and stress starts to wear on your nerves—the housekeeper might come into the room at any minute, or else the fumes from the fire might waft toward the landlady's room.

Gorats, incidentally, did not attempt to educate us in science alone. In those days, the most beloved poet of the young generation was Nadson, and my cousin would often read his poems to us.[24] He read with heartfelt conviction, tenderly and with great feeling, so as to create a mood of melancholy, a sense of longing for things near and dear. This melancholy, however, did not destroy the beauty of the work.

Among the students there were groupings known as *zemliachestva*, which brought together young people who hailed from the same part of the empire. Our circle often threw parties, at which poets of our generation, like Frug,[25] Minskii,[26] Fet,[27] and others, would read from their work. Grand balls and concerts were also held to benefit the Higher Women's Courses, and some of the best opera singers of the Mariinskii Theater would perform at these galas. I volunteered as a stage manager for one of the balls. My duties consisted of waiting in the wings and looking after the needs of the artists. When they exited the stage, I applauded them with all my heart and expressed my admiration. Usually, I had to watch the singers from high up in the gallery, but now here I was looking at them face-to-face—Koriakin,[28] the beautiful Mravina,[29] Savina,[30] and Strepetova![31] I brought them platters of fruit and pleaded with them to take one more curtain call for the audience. When they smiled at me, I was beside myself with rapture . . .

I recall that after the concert Savina sold autographed picture postcards of herself to benefit the Courses. She charged twenty-five rubles apiece. One of the young girls at our Courses was exceptionally pretty, and she managed to bring in a fabulous sum that night, outstripping even Savina. This girl was a real Russian beauty, lively and witty with a pert, upturned little nose, her light brown hair tied back in two thick braids, and bright blue eyes sparkling with intelligence. She was selling kvass at the ball that night, and managed to persuade the audience members that her kvass was tastier than champagne.[32] People were enchanted by her, and so they believed her, paying as much for her kvass as if it were real champagne.

VII

The first school year flew by. We used the spring recess to study in earnest for our five upcoming exams. Besides the printed lecture notes, we were required to read a whole stack of books for each subject and memorize a great deal as well. I had lots of energy in those days and worked with great enthusiasm.

There was only one unpleasant moment during the exams—when you drew your number and looked at the list on the table to determine which question you were supposed to answer.[33] At first, I would see spots dancing before my eyes, and then my mind would just go blank; it seems as if you can't remember anything or even understand what's being said—such an awful state to be in! But in due time the blood begins to flow back to the head, and once again everything you know about the given question comes back to you. Now you can walk up to the table to answer, fully confident in your knowledge, without the slightest fear. With time, the exams only became easier.

In my opinion, the time of year usually set aside for exams is a bad one. Psychologists should look into this question. Springtime usually excites the nerves of young people, producing all sorts of stresses and strains, and not all students are up to the task of concentration. The morning hours were the time of my most intense work, and I recall how much I suffered on account of all the yelling and screaming from the vendors who frequented the courtyards of Vasilevskii Island (of course, in the center of the city, where the wealthy homes were located, the vendors were not allowed to disturb the fine folk). Sharp cries mixed with grating melodies that were literally torture on the ears. No sooner would one vendor fall silent than another one would start up. The shouting stayed with me throughout the entire day. Boys calling out: "Matches here! Papers! Matches!" Women in falsetto voices: "Herring! Dutch herring!" Tatars in their bass voices: "Robes! Robes!" A tradeswoman: "Live fish, live fish!" And yet another salesman: "Floor mops! Floor mops!" and so on and so forth.

We were given only five days to study for the physics exam. On the first day the weather was so beautiful that it was simply unthinkable to sit at home. I talked my roommate into taking our books to the island, so that we could study in the fresh air.[34] She raised no objection, and so we set off. As it happened, we spent a glorious morning in the very lap of nature without so much as opening our books. Later, we had to make up for lost time and cram all night long, fortifying ourselves with several glasses of strong tea.

The exam period was drawing to an end when we received news that struck the students, professors, and our poor Nadezhda Vasil'evna like a thunderbolt. We were young, and young people can always cope better with bad tidings, but the news hit Nadezhda Vasil'evna especially hard. On one of those glorious May days, we read in the evening edition of the *Pravitel'stvennyi Vestnik* (Government Herald), in tiny print on page four, in the section

that dealt with events of the day, that the Higher Women's Courses
would henceforth be closed, pending further notice. The news fell on
Petersburg like a bolt out of the blue, and students from all around
the city began to gather at the Courses in large crowds. Nadezhda
Vasil'evna was already there, along with many of our professors.
The crowds got themselves worked up, made a great deal of clatter
till late into the night, and then simply went back to their homes.
The following morning a delegation set off to see the government
minister, but nothing came of their efforts. At the ministry it was
explained that the Courses would not be closed down just yet, but
no new incoming students would be allowed to register. Next year,
then, we would have students in the three upper-level grades, and
the year after, two, until we had all graduated from the Courses.
My year was to be the last class admitted. It seems that certain
circles were unhappy with the liberal nature of our Courses, which
were quite popular among the intelligentsia; it was thus decided to
weed out the seditious elements and start the Courses anew, with a
specially appointed director and a mandatory dormitory to house
the students. And so it was that my first year of studies, which had
begun so joyously, ended most unhappily.

VIII

After my last exam, I began preparing to go home for the summer.
All of the terrible reversals of fortune that had preceded my departure
were now forgotten. I was joyous and happy all the way home. I felt
that I had changed beyond all recognition.

That night on the train I didn't sleep one bit; I was too excited in
anticipation of my arrival. Two hours before the train was scheduled
to arrive, I was already set to disembark. I wanted to see my sister as
soon as possible, and I was certain that she would be waiting at the
station, since I had told her when I was to arrive. With a few final
bumps and shoves, the train pulled into the station. My eyes searched
the crowd for my beloved sister. I so desperately wanted to throw
myself around her neck and kiss her forever! I spotted her from afar
while she was anxiously looking about in all directions, searching
for me. I called to her, and she came running. I saw a look of horror

in her eyes. "What's wrong, Polechka?" I asked. "What happened to you?" she whispered. "Your face is all black, covered in soot. It's impossible to even kiss you!" "Big deal!" I cried, and began kissing her, dirtying her face with soot.

Our parents were already at the dacha for the summer. My sister made me wash up at the station, and then we headed home. Mamasha—cheerful and friendly as always—greeted me warmly. Papasha, in a more reserved tone, expressed his satisfaction that I had changed for the better.

I had indeed matured in the past year, not only in terms of my appearance but inwardly as well. I had lost my veneer of provincialism. I had lost weight, grown taller, and gotten paler—paleness, incidentally, was quite in fashion in Petersburg in those days; there was even an expression in use at the time: "a striking paleness." It so happened that rosy cheeks lent one a rather provincial look. I had already been told of these changes at the end of the school year by some of my Petersburg acquaintances. I had grown more agile as well, and I had even learned how to leap on and off a moving tram car, which we regarded as quite a sign of skill and dexterity. In a word, I had become a real Petersburger.

At this time my parents were staying at Bel'mont, where a limited number of dachas were rented out to the same families from the same bourgeois set year in and year out. I never really had much sympathy for this class of people: they possessed nothing that attracted me to them and much that quite simply repelled me. I always instinctively kept my distance from our Bel'mont neighbors, despite the fact that my parents and my sister were on friendly terms with them. For their part, our neighbors were aware of my feelings, and I didn't remain in their good graces for long. I took some pride in the fact that I did not conform to their image of an ideal young woman. The family that lived next door to us provided me with ample opportunity to observe bourgeois psychology in action. Their most defining feature was their desire to flaunt themselves before others. To call attention to themselves was their goal in life. *Madame* was tall, with a heaving bust; she wore fancy dresses and draped herself in expensive jewelry at all hours of the day. Some time later it came out that half her stones were fake, and even her closest friends could not forgive her this. But with the help of her diamonds, Madame was able to fool the foreign upper crust. Bustling about Europe from spa to spa, she stayed at all the finest first-class hotels, passing herself off as a countess.

Puffed up and arrogant, this lady usually appeared in the company of her daughters, the three Graces, as we called them. They were also puffed up and big-bosomed, and made a point of speaking French instead of Russian. To round out this portrait I should also mention the French governess, whose slender waist, pushed-up bust, loud speech, and ringing laughter made quite an impression on the dacha crowd. I particularly remember how Madame, her three daughters, and the governess would squeeze themselves into a four-person carriage and ride off into the city. They wore wide-brimmed hats with bunches of flowers and luxurious dresses cinched tightly at the waist. The girls' shoes were especially unique, and I recall that I was quite taken with them at the time: black worsted wool, with thin stripes and fastened with small buttons. All three wore light blue stockings. The governess was dressed more modestly than the ladies, but she too wore a large hat. As I recall, the ladies rode into town in their carriage, while the head of the household would leave for work in the city every morning on foot. (I almost forgot about him, perhaps because he played such a small role in the family.)

In our family we had no idea that in a "respectable" household the help was supposed to wear a lace cap. But across the way, our neighbors' servants would wear gloves while serving at the table. Our neighbors would host grand balls in the winter. Even during my years at the gymnasium, my parents would try to persuade me to attend, but I could not be budged. The guests at these balls were treated to expensive fruits. I remember one story about how the old man got angry because his guests were digging into the costly Duchess pears without hesitation. He flew into a rage and ate several handfuls himself—"Well, it doesn't matter now," he said. "The money's already spent!"

In those days, fashionable ladies would freely slip French words into their Russian conversations, as if to give the impression that they could not find the proper Russian words to express their thoughts. I constantly was subjected to phrases like: "Well, you know, Polechka, *entre nous soit dit*—she's pretty ugly."[35] Or: "You know, Polechka, *entre nous soit dit*—she's just living with him." Once she had gossiped about all her acquaintances to her heart's content, the speaker, sighing deeply, would invariably conclude her conversation with the well-loved phrase: "*C'est la vie*, Polechka, *au revoir!*" At times our neighbors would quite unexpectedly switch from French to Yiddish. Sometimes, if a young girl would happen to stroll into our grove with her governess, one of the neighbor girls would start praising her beauty: "*Vous savez, Madame, la petite est vraiment charmante, mais je vous dis, char-mante!*"[36] And then to herself, in Yiddish: "Oh, what a slut!"

I remember that I especially enjoyed taking walks in the summertime. Two or three mornings a week we would set out for the outskirts of town—some fifteen or twenty versts distant. The group that I organized consisted of a dozen or so young people. Gradually, though, the group became smaller, and by the end only three or four of us were left. I remember we got lost once and returned home that evening by a completely roundabout route. To shorten the distance we had to cross the ford of our beloved little river, the Vileika. At that time of year the river flows very swiftly, and the current pulled the shoes right off my feet and swept them away. I made my way home barefoot and completely soaked, and, what's more, I had to walk through the clearing in the grove where the Bel'mont ladies sat in their circle, carrying on their delicate conversations concerning some rather indelicate behavior. Just imagine their amazement when I appeared before them—barefoot, in a wet dress clinging to my body, my hair unkempt, and still merry all the same, laughing heartily! The ladies could barely conceal their embarrassment. My family tried to drop hints that perhaps I didn't always conduct myself with suitable propriety, but I would always reply: "If you listen to what everybody else has to say, you'll wind up carrying the donkey on your back!" I can't remember where I dug up this bit of wisdom.[37]

The natural beauty of Bel'mont is comparable to Pushkarnia or Kuchkuryshka, where I spent the last years of my youth. Not far from Bel'mont, on the opposite side of the river, is the Pushkino estate, which belonged to the son of the great poet. Pushkin's daughter-in-law just recently died, only a few years ago. After her death, the house and grounds, along with all the family portraits and other relics, were turned over to the Russian Society, which in 1937 hosted an interesting exhibition in Vil'na to commemorate the poet's centenary.[38]

While we were staying at Bel'mont, I also enjoyed boating. Our

Vileika may have run shallow in the autumn, and the bed was rather rocky, but nonetheless its banks were quite beautiful. Every evening, I would go boating with my old friend "Onegin." He rowed calmly and with such confidence, and I made it seem as if I were helping him. Since boating carried with it a certain amount of risk—there were, after all, large rocks beneath the surface—we felt ourselves quite the heroes. There was only one boat at the pier, and during our outings I felt as if I were on a desert island. I would spend the entire day in eager anticipation of our evening excursions. On quiet, starry nights I loved to lie down in the boat with my hands behind my head, watch the billions of stars that flickered in the dark blue heavens, and listen to the gentle splash of the oars in the deep silence.

We spoke not a word to break the charm of the summer night, and afterward, just as silently, we left the boat on the shore, mooring it to the pier, and walked home, holding hands. In this way alone did the closeness we felt toward each other make itself known.

IX

My sister somehow tricked me into going to the Swiss Garden, located not far outside the town. This was where the boring townies entertained themselves, whiling away the time over a glass of beer. The garden was owned by a local brewer, who brought in balladeers from Germany to entertain his customers and keep them satisfied with their lighthearted little songs (in those days we placed great value on all things foreign). This particular genre was very much in fashion at the time, and lots of people came.

At the garden, my sister met up with a whole group of young people; among them was M.M.V., to whom my sister introduced me. This encounter would prove to play an enormous role in my life, and so it is no wonder that I can still recall it in all its details. My new acquaintance's gray eyes, with their long, upturned lashes, made quite the impression on me. From the way he looked at me, with such amazement and intensity, I understood that I had made an impression on him, as well. The first glance, the first sensation of some sort of surging happiness making itself felt—these are the decisive moments in a person's life.

A secret bond formed between us. This was our first and at the same time, I think, most genuine declaration of love. A declaration without words! We both felt as if the most important thing had already been said. For the next three years we would meet, write to each other, go without seeing each other for a period of time, and then be suddenly reunited: all this without ever once speaking of love.

My sister told M.M. that we were preparing to take a trip to our hometown of Bobruisk to visit our aunts and grandfather, and that we already had free first-class tickets. M.M. said that he too had a free rail ticket, to Riga. In those days, some of the railroads were owned by wealthy Jewish financiers, and we would receive free tickets from the railroad employees. My sister suggested to M.M. that he exchange his ticket and travel with us to Bobruisk rather than Riga. He agreed at once. It turned out that he had relatives in our town and that we were practically neighbors. I immediately guessed that his change of mind had nothing to do with his relatives. We, of course, stayed at the garden until the performances were over. It was a pity that it had all ended so quickly and that we now had to return home. I was comforted, though, by the thought that my new acquaintance would most likely change his ticket. And this is precisely what happened— two days later we all met at the train station. Our younger sister, Idochka, came with us. M.M. brought his little brother, who rode with us in our compartment.

Seeing that we were traveling first-class, the conductor mistook us for wealthy folks and shouted at the porter, who was carrying someone else's suitcases into our compartment: "You idiot! Can't you see that they're traveling together as a family?"

***

I had left Bobruisk as a six-year-old child, after my mother's death, and had never been back since. My sister must not have notified our relatives that we were coming, because no one met us at the station. As luck would have it, we managed to find two broken-down old droshkies—a pair of rickety, old-fashioned carriages that once upon a time must have belonged to some landowner but were now harnessed to a pair of old nags. We had to travel a couple of versts from the train station into town. We tried to explain to the driver where we needed to go. It took him awhile to figure it out, but then, finally, he exclaimed: "Oh, I get it, I get it! You want to go to Gruncha's!" Everyone called my aunt by her first name, even drivers. What's more, she was considered one of the wealthiest women in town. She was Grandfather's oldest daughter and had been married off to a well-to-do merchant from Gomel. Grandfather, it seems, had exchanged *yikhes* (lineage) for money. Grandfather and his in-laws reminded me of characters from an Ostrovskii play.[39]

At first, my aunt had lived with her husband's family, but soon the young merchant branched out from his father's business and began to trade on his own. Hoping to get rich as quickly as possible, he managed instead to lose all his money and had to turn to my father for help. He had plenty of plans and schemes—each one supposedly more brilliant than the next. After a series of unsuccessful attempts, he settled on the barrel business (to be more precise, the wooden staves used to make barrels) and soon managed to acquire a tidy sum of money. He settled down in Bobruisk and lived quite nicely. A poor man made good, he decided to rub it in other people's faces and build himself a mansion. You could count the number of fine houses in Bobruisk on your fingers—there were only three or four of them. Aunt Grunia lived in one with her three children; her husband was always out of town on business trips. Our grandfather and his wife lived in a small house on the grounds. The old woman still wore the same cap that I remembered from my childhood, with what I think was the very same embroidered ribbon. She had hardly changed a bit. Grandfather, too, was still as handsome as ever. Aunt Polia was around twenty-six or twenty-seven but was already regarded at the time as an old maid. She played preference very well, and even vint. She played only with men, and with the best card players in town.[40]

The citizens of Vil'na considered their city to be a real metropolis. My sister, for example, thought that there was not a finer city in the whole world. The hospitality of provincial towns, however, is proverbial. Everyone knows that the smaller the town, the friendlier and more heartfelt is the greeting shown to guests, especially those from big cities. Since I was a student from Petersburg, I was looked upon as some sort of foreign wonder. And for his part, M.M. was a student in the medical faculty at Dorpat.[41] No wonder that our visit brought all of Bobruisk to its feet, and we were constantly in demand as guests and visitors.

My sisters and I stayed with Aunt Grunia, an intelligent woman who conducted herself with the dignity befitting a lady. M.M. stayed with his uncle, who lived in a large house that was old and in terrible disarray. The house was full of all sorts of relatives, who were all dependent on the old man. Bobruisk did not yet have paved roads or sidewalks, and without streetlights it was impossible to take even one step outside in the evenings.

We stayed only ten days, but the whole time I felt as if I were in a haze. I would start worrying in the early hours of the morning: who knows, I thought, whether M.M. will pay us a visit today? I was certain that he would come; it couldn't have happened any other way. As we pressed our hands together to say farewell each evening, I could feel that he was making an unspoken promise to come again the following day. But all the same, my soul was anxious. In the hours before lunch, I was simply beside myself. Nothing held my interest. I could barely listen to what people around me were saying, and I was amazed that others could feel so joyous when M.M. was not with us. I grew silent and taciturn, and, though it was awkward to act so, I could not bring myself to snap out of it. And yet each day, just as the time for afternoon tea drew near, M.M. would appear. The burden that had weighed so heavily on me would disappear the minute he arrived, and I would eagerly take part in the general laughter and merriment. I was aware that this sudden transformation that came over me must have been strikingly apparent to all around me, but I simply could not suppress the joy that bubbled up inside me. I still remember the special look M.M. would give me when Aunt Polia (with whom M.M. had been friends since childhood) would say something flattering to him about the two of us!

It was clear to everyone that a romance had begun between the two of us. It seemed to me that everyone was all smiles and happiness for us. M.M. conducted himself with great restraint, treated everyone with equal grace, and paid attention to everyone. He stood out from the others by his intellect and good manners. He was a true gentleman, and I always felt comfortable in his company.

X

Our ten days in Bobruisk flew by in a single, happy flash. Of course, we departed together, as well. M.M. was staying in the dacha settlement of Erusalimka, on the banks of the Vileika. Our balcony looked out upon a large meadow and a little bridge that spanned the river. I knew that M.M. always came by between seven and eight o'clock, and so I would make certain to be at home at that hour, seated on the balcony with a book in my hand. I could recognize his figure, even from far off, while he was still on the little bridge. Once I saw him, I could no longer concentrate on my book, and so I only gave the appearance that I was reading. Afterward, we would spend several hours in lively conversation and often went out for a stroll. I always felt in a good mood with M.M. by my side. Everyone noticed this—perhaps my sister and my parents were already whispering about this among themselves. You see, they all had but a single thought constantly in mind: the girl is growing up, sooner or later she'll have to get married. Of course, no one talked to me about this! They were all afraid to broach the subject, knowing my rather skittish character. I myself was as far from thinking about marriage as I'd ever been. I felt happy in M.M.'s company, and I needed nothing more than that.

The Markuciai estate was located in our little town of Bel'mont, next door to Pushkino, and there, in a large gentry house, lived the R. family (the two brothers I've already had occasion to mention). The R. family was of the intelligentsia, educated and cultured, with the finest traditions rooted in their very flesh and blood. The young generation, in this respect, did not lag behind their elders. In the R. house there were often discussions on societal questions and literary themes. The women of the older generation gave the impression of biblical matriarchs, and the grown-up sons treated their mothers with great esteem. Among the young people there were a number of musicians with excellent ears. I loved to spend time with that family, and they welcomed me with open arms. M.M. had gone to gymnasium with some of the R. family, and he too frequented the home.

XI

In my younger days we loved to dance, though dances were not as common then as now. In those days, young people came together, principally, for the conversations and discussions, to exchange ideas. Dances, however, were an opportunity for us to show a sign of favor to those we liked. We avoided dancing simply for the sake of dancing, or dancing with just anyone who happened to show up; even if your partner proved to be a splendid dancer, we regarded such a pairing as a punishment of sorts. With just one look at a dancing couple, it was possible to pronounce a definitive diagnosis as to whether they liked each other or not.

Almost at the very end of my stay in Vil'na, M.M. got the idea of inviting me, the R. brothers and their sister, and some other folks to his dacha. As always, we joked a lot and argued, too. One of the R. brothers sat at the piano and played a waltz. We threw ourselves into the dance, though my head was already swimming from an excess of sensations. I don't know why, but I suddenly felt the urge to play a little trick on everyone. Right at the very height of the waltz, I stopped dancing and turned white as a sheet. Then, as if I had lost all my strength, I fell against my partner's arm and, with his help, barely managed to drag myself to the sofa. I lay down motionless, with my eyes closed. I was so into my role that I didn't even have to pretend—it really seemed as if I were done for. Confusion mounted in the circle, everyone was alarmed, everyone huddled round, someone felt my pulse, and suddenly I heard M.M.'s loud and anxious voice: "Well, what are you all crowding round her for? Back away—her blouse needs to be unfastened, I'll bring some water straightaway."

At this point I regretted what I had done. I leaped up from the sofa and confessed that it had all been a joke. One of the guests could not forgive my little trick for quite a long time to come. This was M.M.'s cousin—an unmarried girl who often stayed with his parents. She saw in him a future fiancé, and M.M.'s feelings toward me made her very uneasy. She came to despise me, thinking me an awful little flirt. But she soon took comfort in finding herself a suitable match and got married.

M.M. had four younger sisters. The oldest—a gymnasium student—right away became infatuated with me, in a schoolgirl way. The minute she saw that I was chatting with some other man, she would start fretting over her brother. She would look imploringly at me, as if to say: "You won't find anyone better than M. in the whole world, and no one will love you as much as he!" She was constantly on guard, ready to scratch out the eyes of anyone who spoke ill of me or anyone who might try to court me.

Summer always passes by quickly, especially when you live in a state of joyous excitement, and so the time soon came for us to leave. M.M. was with us on the road: we were to travel together as far as Luga, where he was to change trains for Dorpat. There were lots of young people in the wagon car; we talked a lot, but about serious topics.

M.M. was to change trains at six o'clock in the morning. I was unable to calm my agitation. I had grown accustomed to seeing him every day. It hurt in the very pit of my stomach, and though the feeling gradually subsided, I could not muster a single word. When the train stopped in Luga, those passengers heading to Dorpat began exiting the wagon.

"M.M., you'll be late, we're already in Luga!" I said with some alarm in my voice. But he didn't seem to care, he just smiled and wrapped himself up in his coat, as if he were cold. Then we gazed happily into each other's eyes and smiled. I realized that he intended to escort me all the way to Petersburg. We talked for another five hours, and then, finally, we arrived in the cold, unwelcoming city. M.M. brought me to my house and then set out for the hotel. He left Petersburg that same evening. Before his departure, we stood together in my room for a long time, facing each other. I make no secret of the fact that I was close to tears. I didn't want to part. God knows where my strength and self-assuredness had gone. Nevertheless, pressing my hand, he asked permission to kiss me. I did not consent, and he left chagrined. I realized that our parting had gone badly, and this thought tortured me for a long time to come, though some time later I did the very same thing again.

Mamasha would often remark about me: "Andzia can be very charming when she wants to, but unfortunately she seldom wants to!" Such is a woman's capriciousness; sometimes it is not easy to make sense of our own feelings. It is almost as if there were two "me's" in my younger days—the summer me, carefree and loving life, and the winter me, serious, discontented, with a tendency toward self-criticism and soul-searching. I've often reflected on the inconsistencies in my character. Like all girls, I felt that to love and be loved was the deepest need of the human soul, but I wanted to be loved for my inner qualities, and not for a pretty exterior. I instinctively feared any bursts of passion that might muddle my head, and I staunchly guarded my person and my chastity—for the time being.

To love a long time, to wait patiently, even though you're all atremble inside—this is what I thought true love was. It seemed to me that love was something that had to be put to the test. A careless attitude, even if only toward a kiss, seemed to me a profanation of love.

I've suffered much in my life, trying to make sense of difficult problems. To think less and to live in carefree fashion—such is the wisdom of the world. But the philosophy of Gorats, my teacher, was of a different sort—"A thinking person must suffer."

XII

The day after my arrival I returned to my beloved Courses. Familiar faces flitted about, kursistki greeted one another, but there was not as much noise and commotion as last year, when the lecture halls were filled with first-year students. With sadness I looked at the enormous lecture halls, and at our own Nadezhda Vasil'evna, who had aged ten years in the last twelve months. We were all serious and businesslike, and set about to our studies with redoubled energy.

So as not to waste time commuting to the Courses, I decided to take leave of my roommate and move to Vasil'evskii Island. I ended up in a rather poor room in a courtyard, across from a stable, with windows level to the pavement. The room was so damp that the walls dripped moisture. My friends insisted that I needed to light the stove more often. I asked the landlady about it and paid her for the fuel in advance, but she lit the stove only one time. Overcoming my embarrassment with great difficulty, I reminded her of our arrangement. She burst into my room, her face twisted with rage, hurled five logs that crashed onto the floor, and yelled: "Are you really cold, Anna Pavlovna? I'm astonished!" That was the last time she lit the stove. Still, I stayed there till the end of the school year. I hated moving to a new apartment.

I had not broken all ties with Roza, although she was the complete opposite of me. I was a typical female student: not for nothing had I tried so hard to enter the Courses. I firmly believed that within these walls I could satisfy my thirst for knowledge, that scholarship would help me find the path toward independent, ideal, useful work, that I could live according to the dictates of my conscience. Did I find this path? It's hard to give a straight answer to that question. One thing is clear: the time I spent in the Courses played an enormous role in my life, and if, in later years, I did not muddy myself in the muck of life, I attribute that to the Courses. In fact, I hold dear the memory of the Courses to this very day. Looking back on the long path of my life, I realize now that those years kindled an inextinguishable flame in my soul. Now I am at peace, and the flame will die out with me. It's amazing, though. Only four years, but what an enormous influence they had on the entire course of my life!

I lived very comfortably on Vasil'evskii Island. I felt that I was in my own element. During my second year in Petersburg, I became a great lover of music, particularly the opera. I was simply infatuated with the Mariinskii Theater, with its extraordinary orchestra, comprised entirely of true artists; with the chorus, whose equal I have never heard anywhere in Europe; and with its wonderful soloists, who were constantly shuttling back and forth on tour to all corners of the world. The more you listen to your favorite opera, the more treasures you find within it. While listening to music, I could reach the point of religious ecstasy.

Most of the time I went to the opera with my girlfriend Roza. We would both sit there spellbound, tightly pressing each other's hands during the saddest moments. At that time, such artists as Figner[42] and Mikhailov,[43] Medea Figner,[44] Mravina, Koriakin, Stravinskii,[45] and Ol'gina[46] were at the height of their fame. International celebrities came to Petersburg as well—Masini,[47] Cottone,[48] the Reszke brothers from Poland,[49] Melba,[50] and Ferni-Germano,[51] for whom the opera *Carmen* was written. Foreign guests usually performed in the so-called Italian Theater, but sometimes they were invited to perform at the Mariinskii.

The first to appear onstage at the Mariinskii were the Figners. Figner happened to be the brother of the famous socialist revolutionary, who was, at that very time, languishing in the Schlüsselburg fortress.[52] His Italian wife, Medea, appeared together with him. These artists' exceptional musical abilities and talented acting gave audiences enormous pleasure. Medea was an attractive, dramatic soprano, and Figner was possessed of a soft tenor voice that could penetrate one's very soul. Both of them had mastered their voices magnificently. I'll never forget their performance in *Otello*. I remember the scene where the title character stands behind a column watching Iago, who's holding Desdemona's handkerchief in his hand. Shaking with jealousy, Otello sings, as if to himself: "God, soothe Thou, my sufferings!"[53] I was moved by the artists' emotions, by their sufferings: their talents were so great!

One question often troubled me. Must an opera singer strive to perfect his acting? I wondered about this, particularly in regard to Chaliapin, of whom I was a great fan from the very start of his career. The last time I heard him was in Paris, in 1931, in the role of the miller in *Rusalka*.[54] His acting impressed me so much that his singing receded into the background. I don't mean to say, of course, that Chaliapin should have toned down his acting, but rather that an opera should be staged along different principles than a play—to lend it, perhaps, a feeling of harmony. You always listen to a great singer with delight, even if he is a poor actor. Take Masini, for example. He was completely uninterested in acting. When he started to sing, he would always strike the exact same pose: his leg on a chair, right in the middle of the stage, with his hand on his knee—and thus he would remain until the very end of the aria. We always listened to him with our eyes closed. It was astounding, the ease with which he reached the very highest notes and how long he could sustain his phrases; his endless improvisations on a theme also captivated audiences. It simply took a listener's breath away. Music is able to bring a person into a state of ecstasy, and even now it can do this to me. I would have to say, paraphrasing Pushkin: "To music all ages, young and old, surrender!"[55]

It was not easy, however, for us to attain this pleasure during our student years. The only tickets available for the likes of us were for the gallery, and in the very back rows, no less. These tickets sold for anywhere between twenty and fifty kopecks, but there were lots of takers. The box office opened at eight o'clock in the morning, but in order to get these tickets, you had to arrive no later than six o'clock, and even then there would be a crowd fifty deep. Students did not go for the one-ruble seats, and because the number of cheap tickets was limited, not everyone standing in line could be certain of getting one. A half hour before the box office opened, students would pass around a basket filled with folded pieces of paper with numbers on them. Everybody would draw a number, which indicated your place in the queue. There were usually six hundred to seven hundred numbers, but sometimes as many as a thousand. The first hundred, of course, were the luckiest ones; anyone who drew a number in the six hundreds or seven hundreds or higher might as well go home, because it was clear that they would never reach the head of the line. Each number entitled the holder to purchase two tickets. Besides the students, there were always scalpers hanging about. They would sell tickets right before the show, on the sly, at triple the price.

In order that I might be at my post in line at six in the morning, I had to wake up at five o'clock. Without any tea, without any food, and hastily dressed, I would dash from Vasil'evskii Island to the Mariinskii Theater—about an hour away by foot. I don't know which was worse, the autumn fog or the winter cold. It was so cold that you had to stamp your feet the entire time you were in line, so they wouldn't go numb. But we were never bored—we passed the time with jokes and conversation. Occasionally, there were conflicts with the police, who were apprehensive about large gatherings and were constantly on the alert.

In the end, out of all the throngs of young people standing by, only about 150 lucky folks would wind up with tickets. Even then, I felt I could truly relax only after I was comfortably seated in the theater and with a ticket for the next day's performance already in hand—even if it was for the same opera. I must have heard every opera at least fifteen times, and the more I went, the more I reveled in each melody. Sometimes, after I'd come home from the theater and was lying in bed, I would try to recall a particular melody and couldn't.

And then all of a sudden, in the middle of the night, I would wake up and I could hear the aria within me, in all of its nuances. I was afraid to fall back asleep, for fear of forgetting it.

I was a great music lover, which explains why I held on to my damp little room for so long. My landlady's friend was one of six young engineers who had taken part in the reconstruction of the Mariinskii Theater. These engineers had a pair of reserved boxes in the gallery set aside for them: one rather ordinary, and the other with upholstered seats. They took turns sharing these seats among themselves. I'll never forget the time our landlord knocked at my door (his workroom was next door to mine) and asked if I would like to go see *La Traviata* tomorrow with a female acquaintance of his.[56] I was beside myself with joy. More often he would offer me tickets to the ballet, but at that time I did not particularly care for the ballet and often declined. Of course, I could go to the opera endlessly.

Once *Evgenii Onegin* was playing, with Figner, Iakovlev, Mravina, and Ol'gina—my favorite cast—and though I'd seen the opera so many times already, I just couldn't rest easy. I wanted to go again, but there were no tickets! So I thought to myself, I'll go and try my luck—maybe someone will return a ticket. And so I set out for the theater that evening on a whim. Of course there were no tickets, and it was unthinkable to buy from the scalpers. The performance was set to begin at 8:45 sharp. The halls were starting to fill with people, and everyone had a seat but me. There I was without a seat and without a ticket! When there was a full house, it was possible to sit on the gallery staircase, and so I tried negotiating with the usher. He was a pompous, puffed-up type, with gold lace on his uniform, and he would squeeze you for an exorbitant price no better than the scalpers'—three whole rubles! I stood there quaking in fear, but the usher took no notice of me; oh, he was an excellent student of human nature, to be sure. With the first few strains of the overture, I was completely in his hands. Hurriedly, so as not to miss a thing, I shoved a three-ruble note at him, and with a sinking heart I slumped down onto the steps. I could hardly see a thing, but I didn't need to—most of the time, if I know the opera well, I'll listen with my eyes closed, so that the visual impressions don't distract from the music. I'm certain that those seated in the first few rows of the pit did not experience half the enjoyment that I did, sitting there on the gallery steps. I've had the opportunity to do some traveling in my life, and I've attended the opera in all the major cities I've visited, but I've never seen so fine an ensemble as in Petersburg.

I love symphony concerts and solo performances equally. I remember Hoffmann's first performance at the Nobles' Club—in an empty hall![57] For his next performance, the hall was filled to capacity, with hundreds of people standing throughout the entire concert. Anton Rubinstein played a series of ten concerts that made a particularly strong impression on me, as well. Each concert was, in fact, a double performance, because in the afternoons, before the public concert, Rubinstein played for students—free of charge, of course. These concerts were the highlight of the musical season. Petersburg idolized the composer—and why not? Just one look at him told you he was an extraordinary man. To this day, I can't get past the idea that to be a man of great talent, one has to look like Anton Rubinstein. For those who saw him, his mighty figure was hard to forget: those big, powerful hands with long fingers could make the finest concert pianos in the world tremble and, at the same time, produce the most tender tones imaginable. Rubinstein's playing elicited warm, quiet tears that could ease the soul; one left the concert hall cleansed, renewed, reconciled with life.[58]

XIII

Nothing particularly noteworthy took place during my second year at the Courses. We kursistki had a reputation for our conscientiousness and diligence, and we were all very serious about our studies. The professors used to say that we performed better on our exams than the young men at the university. Each of us felt responsible for everything that took place within the institution's walls, and the honor of our Courses was dear to our hearts. I remember how proud we all were when the Petersburg City Duma commemorated the ten-year career of a female mathematician who had graduated from our Courses. This was Sof'ia Kovalevskaia, a professor at the University of Stockholm. She earned international acclaim and died in the very flower of life.[59]

The internal life of the Courses was extremely well organized. The cafeteria, for instance, was run in exemplary fashion, and the food was always of the highest quality. The kursistki themselves managed the cafeteria, for which they received a small salary. They used to go to the market very early in the morning and buy all the supplies themselves. Student workers also helped in the kitchen and prepared meals. There was a buffet table open round the clock, where one could get a cup of tea, some milk, a bun, and so forth. A friendly, easy atmosphere prevailed in our cafeteria, though unfortunately we were allowed only twenty minutes for lunch. You would barely have time to purchase your ticket and receive your food before the next bell would ring for lecture. We discussed all the important questions of the day in the cafeteria, its walls plastered with all sorts of appeals and addresses. Toward the end of my time in the Courses, the watchful eye of the authorities began to look askance at our autonomy, and finally our little cafeteria was shut down.

My best friend in the Courses, Roza, played an enormous role in my student life, and so I'd like to give a little sketch of her, albeit in abbreviated form. We had studied together in Vil'na, in the same gymnasium, but we had little in common back then. Happenstance brought us together, and I was very much taken with her. Our relationship developed in such a way that I, the stronger and healthier of the two, took on the role of guardian. During our years in gymnasium, my girlfriend was very pretty. The beauty of her brow, eyes, and hair caused you to forget the minor flaws in her features. Her father committed suicide, and after his death Roza left the gymnasium for a year. She returned afterward but was obliged to take her entrance exam once again. These exams were given in the classroom, during lessons. Our handsome teacher, whom I've mentioned before, administered the exams in Russian language and pedagogy. For an entire hour she stood in front of the chalkboard without answering a single question. Neither we nor the teacher could take our eyes off her. After each question her face got redder and her eyes grew bigger. After he'd taken his fill of letting her stew, the teacher himself would give the answer, tersely and in a quiet voice. And so it went until the bell. Of course, he gave her a C.

I recall yet another Roza story from our gymnasium days. Already in the springtime the young women would look forward to wearing their summer hats. In my opinion, a hat is the most attractive part of a woman's dress. My Roza was always the first to don her summer hat. It was a bright and simple straw hat, trimmed with sprigs and wildflowers; it very much suited her bright face and her cornflower-blue eyes. Several of our classmates tried to copy her style, but good Lord, how ugly those hats looked on their heads!

Her blossoming, however, did not last long. Striking blondes like Roza fade quickly, and already in Petersburg, during our student years, her beauty had begun to wane. Roza was in weak health, and moreover she had inherited from her father a certain emotional imbalance. Pessimism, a critical attitude toward other people, misanthropy—these were her characteristic traits. With me she was on good terms, perhaps because I loved her, took pity on her, and looked out for her. I considered it my moral duty to help her as much as I could, but her moods always troubled me.

Once, in fact, as if I could sense some misfortune about to take place, I followed her into the girls' room and found her with a small bottle of poison in her hands. Good thing I wasn't too late! After that, I went with her every day to the clinic where patients with nervous disorders were treated. There she undertook a lengthy cure, which had a very positive effect on her.

Unlike Roza, I felt terrific at this point in my life. I was fascinated by everything, and I loved it all. My appetite was healthy, too. In the mornings, for instance, I would eagerly devour my kalach, while Roza would break off a tiny piece and nibble at it reluctantly. In good conscience I must now confess that I gazed greedily upon Roza's kalach; I might have easily asked her for it, had I not been ashamed of my own appetite.

She and I often visited each other. Sometimes I would invite her to spend the night, and I was delighted when she accepted. As is often the case with nervous people in general, Roza's sleep was intermittent and restless, and so, of course, I let her have my bed, with the pillow and blanket and even my little throw pillow, while I slept on the tattered little sofa. I placed a jacket under my head and covered myself with a threadbare rug. The sofa was too small, so my legs struck against a heavy chair. Despite the discomfort, I slept like a log the whole night through, and in the morning I leaped up from the sofa and asked Roza how she had slept. It turned out she hadn't closed her eyes once, because my little throw pillow was a couple inches larger than what she was used to. Thereafter our paths began to diverge. She took only a few classes our third year and did not take her exams.

Throughout this whole time M.M. and I established a regular correspondence, but his letters to me were short and rather dry; they did not excite me at all but in fact left me rather cool.

XIV

In the summer I returned home once again. Our family lived in Pushkarnia, where the paper factory was located. From that time forward, I spent every summer in Pushkarnia. My sister lived here uninterruptedly for thirteen years. At that time, there were two large houses in the village, and my sister lived in one of them, close by the factory. In the summer she would always have many guests who came from out of town. My sister was a delightful hostess—everyone found her home to be warm, cozy, and friendly. My parents lived in the other house, the so-called palazzo. This was an old, neglected gentry house, with many enormous rooms and a pleasant veranda, from which you could see the small creeks that flowed into the river.

My parents' house stood on the site of an old overgrown garden with many secluded little corners. I was never bored here, and in fact, it was impossible to be bored in the summertime, in the open air, in the countryside, where every path, every sapling was near and dear to me. I have always dreamed of a life close to nature. Even now I believe that if a certain something from that time has been preserved within me still, something that has prevented me from getting bogged down in the muck of life, then I owe it to the saving, ennobling influence of nature.

Unfortunately, we Jews, obliged to live in towns, seldom have the possibility of a prolonged communion with nature. Few of us have ties to those small country places with their beloved paths and little out-of-the-way corners. But I was brought up this way, and I've spent the summers in the very same country spot now for nearly half a century.

The area surrounding Vil'na was always praised for its picturesque beauty, and many referred to our Pushkarnia and Kuchkuryshka (the neighboring estate) as "Switzerland." Indeed, this is a very pretty place, everything here is a joy for the eyes to see: the swift, winding brook with its picturesque banks; the hills of budding rye, rich with all the shades of gold and green; the well-maintained forest, which one can walk across so lightly and softly, as if it were a carpet; and the wide, open horizon, edged with trees that seem so densely clustered. Here were my most beloved places, places I could never pass by with indifference; especially dear to me was the country road that led from Pushkarnia to Kuchkuryshka.

We lived much more comfortably in Pushkarnia than in Bel'mont; there was no one here but my family. It seemed to me that all the forests, all the beloved little corners and winding paths, all this belonged to me; that the nightingale who made its nest in the tree outside our house sang only for me; that the cuckoo, whose calls echoed in the forest, promised me good things. If I had been asked at the time which I preferred—people or nature—I would have answered unhesitatingly: nature!

XV

In those days young people rarely played sports. Going out for a stroll, boating, croquet, ring toss, and swimming—these were our summertime entertainments. Amateur performances were also popular, and it was then that I came to realize my enthusiasm for them. It so happened that plans for a summer production were under way. The initiator was an acquaintance of ours, T.O. Shabad, who later became a prominent public figure who devoted all his energies to the Jews of Vil'na.[60] At this time he was a medical student in Moscow. He and I had known each other since we were schoolchildren; in fact, my memories of him have to do with a certain incident that reflects rather poorly on me. When we were in gymnasium together, we had been assigned a composition on the theme "The Significance and Usefulness of Railroads." The topic bored me, and I couldn't bring myself to work on it; on the other hand, it proved very much to T.O.'s liking, and he was eager to dive in. In the end, he wrote my composition for me. It was the first and last time in my life I pulled such a trick, and my conscience tortured me for a long time thereafter.

Now, several years after, T.O. and I were reunited in Pushkarnia and spent the summer together. It was his idea to stage an amateur performance with a "troupe" consisting of the organizer himself, my brother, my sister, my little sister's teacher, a male student of our acquaintance, and myself. Having read through a whole series of plays, we settled on a popular comedy that had been performed at the Aleksandrovskii Theater with Savina. The play was called *The Madcap*.[61] We set to work at the end of July. As director, T.O. was up to the task and cast all the roles expertly; everything on our end, however, turned out much worse.

We started to learn our lines and rehearsed every day. Even during our long strolls, we "artists" would break off from the rest of the company and organize rehearsals. Our other friends—there were four of them—would hang around during rehearsals. In fact, they knew all our lines by heart. No sooner would we begin than they would call out in unison, imitating the director's intonation: "Pardon me, princess, that you think we're all a bunch of silly chickens. We can get you chickens! They're easy to come by in the village!" We worked ourselves ragged. The director shouted at us constantly; he was dissatisfied with us, and we wore ourselves out trying to please him. The parts were distributed as follows: I played the lead; my brother played the young man in love with me; T.O. played the father, an old landowner; our student friend played the general; my little sister's teacher, the princess; and my sister, the old peasant woman.

We did not overburden ourselves with rehearsals; on the contrary, we were ready to postpone the performance, since, to tell the truth, we'd been so busy with the set and costumes and so forth. But summer was coming to a close, and it was time to think seriously about completing our work.

Of course, in preparing for my role I tried with all my heart to imitate Savina, but alas! I had managed to reproduce only one detail: I wore exactly the same dress—bright red muslin, with little white polka dots. For the sake of art I even refrained (the only time in my life) from the principle of modesty—I wore a bit of décolletage and short sleeves!

Our excitement grew with every day. Finally, a date was set for the show, and all the costumes were ready. We sent invitations round to everyone we knew. We decided to stage the play on my sister's veranda, and so we removed the front railing of the veranda and set up a prompt box. Our director, though, had made one unforgivable blunder: we had not had a single dress rehearsal in costume.

The mishaps began on the very day of the show. Our "princess" (the schoolteacher) unexpectedly had to go to town for the traditional bride-show, or *smotrina*.[62] We were distraught, and so we threw ourselves on the mercy of Mamasha, trusting in her cleverness and resourcefulness. Mamasha came to our rescue: she went into town and persuaded the fiancé to put off the smotrina for a few hours. Our entire house was in an uproar, and even Dveira—Sister's cook—was as nervous as could be. When asked why she was boiling potatoes at such an inopportune time, she replied, in Yiddish: "For all this madness!" In truth, we needed a potato for the play, when the impoverished countess treats her guest to an "American fruit," as she calls it.

Those of us playing young characters acted without makeup, but we brought a hairdresser in from town to make up the actors playing the "old folks." How funny it was when we all met in costume in the hall! The general wore a student's jacket with epaulettes, and trousers with red calico stripes; he sported a real devil-may-care moustache. The princess—an old woman, with powdered hair and a black lace headdress—carried herself with great propriety. But what had happened to my "Papasha"! T.O. was mumbling his lines so that you couldn't understand a thing—the hairdresser must have glued his beard too high on his face. His arms hung at his sides like loose strings, his whole appearance had changed to the point that he was no longer recognizable: what had happened to his free and easy movements, the lack of affectation that had so captivated us during rehearsals! I laughed till my sides ached and tried to shake some sense into him, grabbed him by the shoulders and started walking him up and down the hall: any minute now he was to go onstage, smiling and affable, and pronounce the well-known opening lines: "Pardon me, princess . . ."

The first bell sounded. I looked out the window: there was a crowd of spectators in the garden, stretching all the way to the fence and beyond; the workers from the local paper factory had come from all around to see the show. It was a real production. We could have even posted up a notice—"The show is sold out!" This gave us courage. After the third bell, the princess strode out onto the stage with her haughty bearing. "Papasha" was supposed to come in behind her; but our "Papasha's" legs were all atremble (from old age, it must have been), and so we had no choice but to push him onto the stage.

We were able to pull off the first few scenes, but all of a sudden, at the very height of the performance, all the actors got their parts confused. A terrible mix-up ensued, and the stage was left empty. The indignant director stormed out of the prompt box. Once again, Mamasha saved the day: she persuaded him to come back to the stage, and the play continued. The audience, fortunately, paid no attention to this incident—they thought the empty stage was just part of the play.

To sum up: our director, T.O., proved to be the worst actor of us all, and my sister, playing the old peasant woman, was the best, even though she didn't know her lines and hadn't participated in the rehearsals. She borrowed a flowered skirt from one of the working women and wore the cook's broad caftan and, on her head, a red scarf with a gold pattern. The moment she stepped onto the stage, she threw herself at the landowner's feet and started howling and wailing, constantly wiping her nose with the end of her scarf and muttering some ad-libbed lines. This was the best scene in the whole show. The audience applauded her endlessly. After the show, supper was served at my parents' house for all our invited guests, and then the dancing began. Incidentally, the workers ended up knocking the fence over from leaning too heavily on it. And thus concluded our little undertaking.

XVI

At the end of summer we parted company: T.O. to Moscow, and I to Petersburg. I returned to my Vasil'evskii Island and found a decent room for myself. I took up lodging with a lady—by the looks of it a very important one—with a stormy past. She had once been the mistress of a grand prince.

Apparently, this lady had a good head on her shoulders, and in her day she had managed to put aside a tidy sum of capital, but now she lived in rather a carefree fashion. She was an attractive woman, though her hair, which she wore in a light, fluffy style, had gone gray.

She had delicate features and a stately bearing. She lived with a woman she took care of, but rented out the other rooms: I took the small room, and the R. brothers took the large, richly furnished study. They had ottomans in their room in place of beds. I was utterly uninterested in my landlady's past, but the R. brothers would sit with her for entire evenings over a cup of tea, while she told them of her bygone glory days, of the balls and galas, the palace intrigues, and so forth.

My room was very cozy, with a comfortable sofa newly upholstered with flowered cretonne, and new curtains hanging in the windows. I converted a card table into a writing desk and fastened picture postcards to a blotter on the side of the desk that leaned against the wall. Sometimes my neighbors would stop by to see me; on those occasions we would take our meal together. My sister would often send me various delicacies: kosher sausage, Swiss cheese, caviar, chocolate, fruit, and cookies. The R. brothers were particularly delighted by these parcels and would devour the lion's share of what was sent. I would set aside another portion for the landlady, too, but whatever food remained would languish on the shelves and spoil—I would completely forget about it.

Once when my girlfriend came to visit, the R. brothers insisted that we dine with them. We agreed, but their room lacked a certain comfort; besides, our hosts treated us with great formality, and it made me uncomfortable. Finally, I could take no more and I suggested that they come back to my room: we brought over the samovar and the food, and once again everything was cheery, informal, and cozy.

In my day, female students would spend the night in male students' lodgings without thinking anything of it. Young people in Petersburg back then weren't afraid of a little gossip. A close female acquaintance of mine, in fact, lived openly with a male colleague of hers, even though she had a husband in Switzerland. I did not judge them, figuring that everybody has the right to live their lives as they see fit. I myself, however, was quite naive and punctilious in my private life. My head told me one thing, but my heart told me something else entirely. We knew a certain student—a handsome young man, a real lady-killer brimming with self-confidence. For some reason I needed a particular book that he had. I asked him several times to lend it to me, and he proposed that I stop by his place to pick it up after classes. I was excited on the way, but as soon as I stepped onto the staircase my heart began to pound. The young man seemed rather disagreeable to me (I don't like those types of people), but at the same time—I must confess—I was afraid of his irresistibility. He had an overly familiar manner in his interactions with women. He was fully confident that no one could resist his charms, and this always annoyed me.

The minute I entered I was struck by his elegant manner. He wore a cream-colored Russian blouse with blue embroidery, which suited him very well and clung closely to his manly chest. Apparently, he was trying to present himself as best he could. He invited me politely to take a seat. At first I refused, explaining that I had to hurry home, but in the end I sat down on the very edge of one of the chairs. He struck up a conversation with me, but the whole time my only thoughts were of getting the book and leaving as quickly as possible. As soon as I found myself back on the street, I heaved a sigh of relief.

I'll recount another minor little episode for what it says about my personality. I spent some time with the family of the well-known doctor N.N., who lived on the Petersburg Side of the city. He was a gynecologist, a handsome man who had enjoyed great success with the ladies. His wife, on the other hand, was most unattractive, but much nicer and more intelligent than he. They were most generous hosts and lived like nobles in a building all to themselves. The doctor was constantly darting back and forth across the city in hired carriages, and every time he happened to see me, or my girlfriend, or the R. brothers on the street, he would wave his arm out the window and shout: "Dinner tomorrow!" This meant that the four of us were obliged to appear at his house, where a Lucullan feast would be laid out for us.[63] These dinners were dazzling, not only in their abundance but also in their refinement, with a whole host of appetizers, pastries, fish, game, and ices.

After dinner the men would retire to the study, and we to our hostess's boudoir. Tea was served at five o'clock, and we would spend an hour or two in the drawing room over the excellent pastries, imported chocolates, and other tasty treats the doctor had ordered. My favorite spot was the rocking chair. On one occasion, we were all chatting merrily after tea. The master of the house stood behind me and gave the chair a good rock. Suddenly, I felt the brush of moustaches on my face; under cover of all the conversation taking place, he had kissed me. The expression on my face changed so that

the doctor, who was apparently accustomed to easy victories, saw
that this was no laughing matter and grew frightened. This episode
had sorrowful consequences: we attended no more of the doctor's
lavish feasts.

***

During my third year in Petersburg, besides the Courses, which I
continued to attend with great interest, I discovered a new passion—
Professor Lesgaft's lectures on anatomy.[64] Lesgaft was a remarkably
talented and multifaceted man: a brilliant anatomist, he was at the
same time an outstanding sociologist, pedagogue, and public figure;
he was able to connect seamlessly every abstract scientific question to
real life. His lectures on anatomy contained a wealth of information
about sociology, psychology, pedagogy, and social science, all of
which he wove together into one systematic whole. Every lecture was
a new revelation of the rationality and method of the universe. After
having listened to his series of lectures it was impossible not to be
filled with admiration for the thoroughgoing orderliness of nature.

A special type of kursistka was formed under the influence of
this remarkable scholar—a "Lesgaftian" was known for her energy,
persistence, hard work, and passion for social causes. The professor
himself led a spartan existence: he worked no fewer than sixteen
hours a day, with the remaining eight devoted to relaxation, sleep, and
spending time with his family. Besides his lectures at the university,
he gave lectures at his house for those who so desired.

His was a two-year course; registration took place right before the
summer recess. With great difficulty, forty people would squeeze into
his tiny little drawing room, with its comfortable furniture, various
unmatched chairs, and a chalkboard. These forty people comprised
a "group." There were four lectures a week for each of the professor's
three groups—two in the morning, from six to eight o'clock, and two
in the evening. We students had to start our workday at six in the
morning twice a week, but Lesgaft did so every day. He dedicated
four hours a day to his home lectures, which he offered completely
free of charge. The audience was made up entirely of male and
female students from the university and the Courses. His favorite
topic was the skeletal system, and he expounded on this subject

with such fervor that he could captivate the entire room. He was especially carried away by the strength of bones and their capacity for resistance. He was enraptured, for example, by the anatomical strength of a ballerina's big toe, which could support and balance an entire body for a span of several minutes.

We listened to each and every one of his lectures with enormous interest. Lectures began at six in the morning, but the students would meet first on the Fontanka from all the various corners of Petersburg; sometimes the walk could take a good hour and a half. I recall one student who slept straight through a full half of the two-hour lecture. You couldn't hide anything from Lesgaft, however, and this particular student immediately fell into his bad graces. Our professor was strict, toward both himself and others. Yet at the same time he was constantly busying himself with matters pertaining to his students, many of whom turned out quite well, thanks to him: some became gymnasium teachers, others took up pedagogical work in accordance with the principles laid out by Lesgaft himself.

At eight o'clock, after the morning lectures, a whole gang of us, together with our professor, would set out for Vasil'evskii Island—the young men on their way to the university, and the young women to the Courses. I confess that on the way back I very much wanted to take the horse-drawn tram, which went almost all the way to the Institute, but like many others I was too shy to do so in front of our professor, for fear that he would tease me on account of such luxury. "What do you think you were given legs for?" he would ask, and stride forward so vigorously that we practically had to rush after him.

XVII

Once again it was the winter holidays, and I traveled home with great happiness. I always loved a change of scenery. Generally, we have a wet winter in Vil'na. After several icy days the thaw and slush sets in, dirty wet snow covers the cobblestones, and the sleighs scrape against the stones. But this winter there was a terrific sleigh path, enough sun to keep us warm, and enough frost to nip at our ears. It was a time to be light in spirit; when you're young, everything is joyous.

As before, my sister was staying outside of town, in Pushkarnia. I remember going to visit her. The children were asleep, and the two of us sat together. As always, my sister was sewing, darning, or mending some children's things, while I told her about my life in Petersburg. The shutters were already closed, and the housekeeper had placed a log in the stove for tomorrow's fire. We were waiting for my sister's husband to come back from the factory before we ate dinner; in any event it was almost nine o'clock and time to turn in.

All of a sudden there was a sound like the ringing of little bells. A loud laugh and a great clatter echoed on the front porch, and a merry group of young people burst in. They headed straight from the cold doorway to the dining room, but my sister directed our guests to the big kitchen, where they took off their shawls, fur coats, and galoshes. In the blink of an eye all the kerosene lamps were lighted, and it became bright and festive. There was no end to the talking, the laughter, and the joking.

My sister sprang to life, bustling about to make everyone feel at home. An extra leaf was added to the dinner table, and the ringing of plates and dishes resounded. All the goodies were brought out of the cupboards, and beverages appeared on the table—vodka, cognac, beer, wine. My brother-in-law found some card players among the guests and, to his supreme satisfaction, got a group together to play preference.

The sad old piano waited its turn: you couldn't have a party without dancing! I glanced at the newcomers. My attention was drawn to one of them, the first man I saw. As it turned out, he sat next to me at dinner, which was very nice for me, and he and I spent the entire evening together. After dinner we danced quite a bit to the sweet strains of our old potbellied piano. We mostly danced the waltz and the mazurka; the dancing lasted till three o'clock in the morning.

Finally, the sleigh drivers, who had been warming themselves in the kitchen, full and contented, pulled up to the front porch. My sister always remembered to feed the drivers well and treat the horses to some oats. The guests started discussing amongst themselves who was going where. I decided to ride into town with them. My new acquaintance carefully helped me into a sleigh and covered my legs with a rug; some other guests sat next to me and across from me. There were not enough seats in the sleighs, and I couldn't believe my eyes that he was not sitting beside me. Everyone laughed at how the passengers' legs were all tangled up, but I alone kept stubbornly silent.

The frozen horses darted and dashed beneath the blows of the tipsy drivers. Suddenly, I felt a strong support behind my back, and all at once I realized he had leaped up onto the runner of the sleigh and was standing behind me. I felt his quickened breathing. We rode like this all the way to town.

The winter festivities continued for three weeks, and we met every day, although he did not come to call on us at home. I grew more and more convinced that he was not only handsome, but smart, intellectual, and, moreover, an exceptionally delightful conversationalist. My new acquaintance began courting me most persistently, as if from that moment on I had become the very center of his life. He said that meeting me had opened up before him a new path in life, one for which he'd been searching for so long. Of course, such words flattered me and it was nice for me to hear—I felt emotions I had never felt before.

New Year's came, and he and I set out with a group of young people for the little town of Pospeshki, outside of Vil'na. My parents had already begun to suspect that something was amiss. They were against my taking part in this excursion, but my sister, as always, came to my aid and set out together with us. Once again we were in the three-horse sleigh, with the little bells jingling, a quiet, frosty night, the field hidden beneath the snow. It was delightful, but frightening too, and my head spun from the nearness of this fellow who was able to hypnotize me with a single glance. No wonder there are so many songs about magical sleighs!

There were about twenty of us, and we stopped at a little inn for a bite to eat, some drinks, and a bit of dancing. On the way back we found ourselves at another inn. We got out and knocked on the shutters for a long time, until finally the owners got up, lighted all the oil lamps, and set the tables, and once again we had ourselves quite a feast. We kept going till six o'clock in the morning.

The winter holidays passed by quickly, and once again it was time for train stations and conductors. Having bidden farewell to everyone, I looked around for my new friend, but he had disappeared somewhere. I thought to myself: "He always makes such strange exits!" And sure enough, when I stepped onto the train, there I found him. He was sitting right across from me, quite calmly. As it turned out, he had decided he was going to escort me back to Petersburg.

My friend spent an evening in Petersburg. From that moment forth, the two of us struck up a very lively correspondence. I would receive three or four large pages, filled with small, neat handwriting. These were not your typical love letters—he wrote about humanity, the social order, the role of the individual in history, of how he burned to achieve great things and how he felt within him the strength to carry them out. At the end of a letter, he usually added that, in order to realize these plans, he needed me to love him as wholeheartedly as he loved me. He felt that with me at his side he could work miracles. He did not demand an immediate response, however, and was prepared to wait patiently. I myself felt that our paths were intertwined, and that we were bound together inseparably.

The letters came once a week, and I would read them in the evenings. They stirred up inside me a whole swarm of thoughts and feelings that were not easy to manage. I was at a crossroads: I was aware that I was still only a student, still just preparing for the life ahead, but the hazy world that opened up before me seemed alluring, it tempted me with bright prospects. With each letter, I would walk around for several days as if I were intoxicated. I had never been able to share my feelings with others and did not like to do so, and therefore all of this was quite hard for me. With each letter I grew more and more certain that his love for me was deep and powerful, and I myself experienced a feeling that I had never felt before. Till then, it occurred to me, I had never truly loved another.

✳✳

Before a month had passed, my friend once again came to Petersburg. In letters, a person cannot help but repeat himself; meeting face-to-face, every word, every glance strikes straight at the soul. But strange to say, a certain anxiety overcame me in his presence. I was afraid of his love and felt a certain sort of insincerity in his words. He seemed different to me in his letters than in person, and I was worried. I didn't say anything to him about my own feelings and emotions. The more impetuous he was, the more inaccessible and distant I became—this just happened of its own accord.

That winter he came to see me several times unannounced. I would arrive home from the Courses to find him in my room. His last trip proved to be the decisive one. After a long and seemingly relaxed conversation about various trivial matters, his voice suddenly changed. He spoke deliberately and with trembling in his voice, and I felt that the critical moment in our relationship had come to pass. He started pacing the room anxiously, back and forth, and then stopped right in front of me, looking deeply into my eyes. I fell silent. It was too much, I could not return his gaze for long and closed my eyes. Unexpectedly, he fell to his knees before me. Seizing my hands and kissing them, he asked me for my love.

I sat there frozen. I don't know how long this went on, but a voice of caution sounded in my soul: "Get hold of yourself, be strong!" Gently and carefully I freed my hands and rested them on the sofa. The conversation was awkward—it was as if all possible topics had suddenly disappeared. His face changed sharply. After sitting for a little while longer, he left. This was our final meeting.

We parted in the springtime, and when I returned home in the summer, I received a letter from him. His writing was very restrained, but he requested that I give him a decisive answer. Since I hadn't seen him or received any letters prior to this, I looked deep within myself and realized that, for my part, this was only a fling, not the love to which my soul had so long aspired, and so, calmly and with a firm hand, I wrote him my refusal.

***

After the winter recess, my studies proceeded at their normal pace, and as before, I attended Lesgaft's lectures. I was not worried about the end-of-year examinations. We lived the lives of diligent students, but sometimes that life was interrupted by political affairs. I would like to tell of one such demonstration.

It was early spring. A memorial service was announced, in connection with the twenty-fifth anniversary of the death of Dobroliubov.[65] Students at all the institutes of higher learning in Petersburg decided to take part, and early in the morning crowds of young people headed for the Volkovo cemetery.

Various delegations brought dozens of wreaths. When we arrived at the cemetery, around eight in the morning, there were thousands of young people at the gates, a crowd roiling like the sea. It so happened that the gates were locked and the police would let no one into the cemetery. Angry youths tried to force their way through the fence, causing a big stir and starting arguments with the police. In the end, only those delegations bearing wreaths were admitted into the cemetery. When the gates were opened and they made their way to the grave, the whole crowd of students, with heads bared, sang "Eternal Memory."[66]

When the delegations returned, cries were heard from the crowd: "Everybody, head to the Kazan Cathedral!" The crowds set off for the center of the city. We made it halfway, but all of a sudden, when we turned onto the Ligovka embankment, Cossacks on horseback appeared, as if they'd sprung from the very earth itself, and barricaded both ends of the street. We found ourselves trapped on all sides. By this time it was about midday and the weather had changed—rain was pouring down, and a cold wind began to blow. We were all hungry, and it was not easy to stand there in the cold and rain, shifting your weight from one leg to the other. But the young people's spirits did not flag, and they stood there for hours on end, loudly singing student songs and revolutionary songs. The police refused to answer any questions; they were waiting for word from Gresser himself, the head of the city administration. Gresser showed up toward evening and left straightaway; he didn't want anything to do with the students. I remember one young man walked up to him and said: "I want to ask you something, confidentially, off the record . . ." Gresser turned away, without even a glance.[67]

It grew dark and we were all chilled to the bone. Finally, some students were permitted to cross the line and buy some bread for the rest. At seven o'clock in the evening, after Gresser had left, a new squadron of policemen arrived; they spread out across the four corners of the square; they started dividing us up into groups of ten, writing down our last names and addresses. The procedure went on until eleven o'clock at night, and several students were detained. After several weeks the expulsions began, and a dozen or so students were expelled from each institution of higher learning.

XVIII

The exams went smoothly, and upon their completion I left for my beloved Pushkarnia. That summer passed by without any performances, without any courtships. The mood was cheerful. I took lots of strolls, read, and went swimming. By the end of August everyone we knew had gone back to town, and only my middle brother and I stayed on in Pushkarnia for the month of September. My brother and I agreed that we would go on longer and longer strolls each day, but that we wouldn't engage in conversation, since he and I had such different interests. And so it was that we would march about for hours, without exchanging a single word. Early in the morning we went swimming in forty-five-degree water; after having swum in water like that, you would feel refreshed for the rest of the day. Afterward we'd part ways. I would take a book to one of my favorite, far-flung corners of the garden, along with four or five big autumn apples, plucked right from the tree. In the evenings, intoxicated by the fresh autumn air and exhausted from our many hours of walking, we would take to our beds and sleep like logs. And so September passed.

In Petersburg I rented the same room from the same landlady as last year. The Courses were empty, even frighteningly so. There was no one there, aside from this year's graduating class.

After an entire year apart, I once again crossed paths with M.M. He had graduated from university, settled in Petersburg, and was working as an assistant to Professor Kernig at the Obukhov Hospital. Kernig was a German who loved the German way of doing things and was eager to take on students who had graduated from the University of Dorpat.[68] Indeed, there were some very accomplished scholars at Dorpat in those days: the professor of anatomy Rauber was particularly renowned, as well as the Shmidt brothers—a gynecologist and a physiologist.[69] M.M. also worked with Professor Otto, a gynecologist in Petersburg.[70]

I've written that M.M. and I had grown apart over time, but this was not so. Quite simply, M.M., having sensed a certain chilliness on my part, had stopped coming to Vil'na, and thus we went an entire year without seeing each other. Now that he'd called on me in Petersburg and we'd spent time together with our friends, it was as if there had been no separation whatsoever. We spent a great deal of time in each other's company, and we went to the theater together. M.M. bought expensive tickets and did not have to "stand guard" in line.

He was always dear, kind, and tender toward me. I liked the nobleness of his character and his gentlemanly ways. Simply put, I loved him with all my soul and always felt that he was the one person with whom I was ready to join my life forever. But over the course of our acquaintance, it so happened—again, through my own fault— that a certain shadow fell over our relations. It is difficult for me to define what exactly the difference was between us. M.M. was always well dressed in his frock coat and white, starched collar, whereas I was used to the Russian blouse, favored by students, which I saw as an emblem of idealism. He wore a winter coat with a long cape and wrap, à la Evgenii Onegin. The coat looked like something a wealthy landowner might wear, even though it had cost him only a few pennies at the Apraksin market.[71] Compared to our young students, M.M. lived grandly, and this seemed to me to be a strike against him, as well as the fact that he did not have a revolutionary outlook and had not spent his student years dreaming of great political changes. But most of all I was troubled, absurd as it sounds, by his love for operetta. Although he would often go with me to the opera, I detected his secret enthusiasm for light music. No matter how much I tried to introduce M.M. to opera and concert music, he continued to frequent the operetta regularly. On one occasion he succeeded in luring me there. *Der Vogelhändler* was playing.[72] The theater was small in comparison to the Mariinskii, but beautiful. It was the audience, though, that stunned me: the front rows were filled with old, bald fellows and ladies made up like young flirts. And above, as well, up in the gallery, the audience looked to be of a similar sort. There were no young people whatsoever. The orchestra played some light, frivolous airs, which grated on my ears, brought up, as they were, on classical music. The play itself was even worse than the music. The final scene, as I recall, went like this: The hero appears, accompanied by a pair of women selling flowers from their baskets. He playfully chucks each one under the chin in turn, singing: "Sibilinka, Serafimka! The heart, you see, is not like a basket—there's no room for two!" It was with great difficulty that I managed to sit through to the end.

There was, it seems, reason enough for disagreement between us. But while I faulted M.M. in my mind, my heart told me something else entirely, and all rational deliberation is powerless before the voice of one's feelings. Despite our differences in tastes, I knew clearly, definitively, and steadfastly that it was M.M. whom I loved, now and to come. Two people need not be alike in every way to spend a happy life together; they need only to respect and love each other. To put it another way, if you can respect and love someone close to you, then together you can build mutual trust, harmony, and a healthy atmosphere for family life.

I often saw my girlfriend Roza. She had stopped attending the Courses and had not prepared for her final exams. The main reason for this was her poor health; she suffered from chronic head pains and insomnia. Once she announced to me that she was going to be married to the elder of the two R. brothers. I was happy for her; she needed to be married and under the guardianship of a loving person.

As before, I attended Lesgaft's lectures and took great pleasure from them. As with last year, the lessons were twice a week and ended at eight o'clock at night. M.M. would usually wait for me at the gates, and we would head to the Andreev confectionery shop on Nevskii Prospekt, near the Admiralty, for coffee and pastries. M.M. did not like to go by foot, so he was constantly taking a carriage—and for this, too, I would fault him. As we left the shop, he'd often ask my permission to hire a cab for us, but I always replied that I would prefer to walk. Of course, after having taken me home, he would hail a horse-drawn cab for himself. Even in such little things we had different tastes.

The time came for examinations, and all of my attention was focused on my work. No matter how much you had studied, it never seemed enough the day before the exam. I had my head buried in my work when a lady appeared. She was the landlady of a fellow student, Sleptsova, and she informed me that the police had conducted a search of the premises the night before and arrested her tenant. Sleptsova had few acquaintances apart from me, though I must confess that I knew very little about her personal life. She was a beautiful girl, very reserved, who had worked very hard in the Courses and stood apart from the rest of us by virtue of her intelligence.

I was terribly agitated when I learned of her arrest. I realized that it was necessary to act at once and make every effort to come to the aid of my fellow kursistka. The first order of business was to send her some food and books. I set out for the city administrator's chancellery, and there I was given the necessary instructions. The officer on duty, who was in charge of parcels, surprised me with his courteous manner and his attentiveness to the prisoner. He readily accepted my parcels and books, and sometimes even letters, adding as he did: "Don't worry, I will try to reach Miss Sleptsova myself and pass on your greetings." I was pleased that everything had gone so smoothly thus far, and began to take the necessary steps to arrange various meetings, but I received no letters from Sleptsova.

My principal objective was to have Sleptsova released on bail; she needed to sit for her final examinations, because the Courses were to be closed this year once and for all. I was more than a little frightened each time I got ready to visit the procurator's office. I tried to dress carefully and borrowed a new coat from a fellow kursistka, one to go with my brown dress. I didn't want to look like a revolutionary. The procurator conducted himself like a brute—he was a malicious man, scornful of revolutionaries. A month and a half went by. I knew nothing of Sleptsova's family circumstances, only that her father had been governor of Tambov and died while she was enrolled in the Courses. Several weeks after her arrest I received a letter from a young male student who wrote that he was Sleptsova's fiancé and asked that I keep him notified of the results of my efforts.

While I was busying myself with Sleptsova's case, I was tortured by various misgivings: what would happen if I should run into the officer through whom I'd been sending packages, and what if he should bow to me? I couldn't very well acknowledge in public the bows of a gendarme officer! But then what if he should take offense and thus do harm to Sleptsova? Fortunately, my fears proved in vain.

On one occasion the procurator presented me with an unexpected proposal. Sprawled in his deep armchair, his legs outstretched and his hands in the pockets of his trousers, he looked me right in the eye, maliciously and contemptuously, and spat through his teeth: "I'll tell you what . . . I'll agree to release your Slep-tso-va, if you put up a thousand rubles' bail. . . . Can you do that? Heh, heh, heh!" He was clearly mocking me, knowing full well that I was in no condition to come up with such an enormous sum.

"Very well, I'll put up the money!" I replied, without hesitation. The procurator glowered at me and said: "In that case, I'll set a date for you. You bring the money and your Slep-tso-va will be waiting in the room next door."

I have no idea how I managed to come up with a quick and decisive response: the desire to free my girlfriend was so great that I was prepared to move mountains. But though I'd promised to produce the money, I could think of no way to actually do so: I simply put all my faith in a miracle.

My instincts did not deceive me: a "miracle" happened!

XIX

Leaving the procurator's office, my spirits sank. Though I knew little of the ways of the world, it was clear that none of my well-to-do acquaintances would give me a thousand rubles. For whole days and nights I racked my brain, trying to come up with a way to obtain this enormous sum. Was it possible to find people who would listen to my story? Was it possible to find people who would care about a poor young thing languishing in prison? I believed that such people existed, but I did not know where to find them.... And then I remembered a certain kind lady—the writer Ostrovskaia, an author of children's stories.[73] I had been a guest in her home several times, and she had impressed me by her sensitivity and the goodness of her character. I knew that she sympathized with young people, and so I decided to turn to her, even though she did not know Sleptsova at all.

My instincts did not deceive me. The minute I told her of Sleptsova's story, Ostrovskaia grew terribly agitated. "Poor girl, poor girl!" she repeated. "We need to help her at all costs. I will try to get hold of some money, but it's impossible to even dream of such an enormous sum!" Such affliction could be heard in her voice that I had to try and calm her down. It occurred to me that it would be wise for us to pay a visit to Nadezhda Vasil'evna Stasova. Why not let these two women sit down together and figure out where to come up with the money needed? After all, two heads are better than one. I knew that neither Ostrovskaia nor Nadezhda Vasil'evna had any money to speak of, but I was sure that they would use all their energies to assist Sleptsova.

We arranged to meet the following day. Ostrovskaia hoped to raise by then a portion of the sum we needed. When I called on her at the appointed time, I found her in a state of joyous excitement; she had managed to borrow five hundred rubles. Encouraged by our prospects, we set out to see Nadezhda Vasil'evna. She greeted us very warmly and sympathetically. We did not have to persuade her. Right away she took to heart the misfortunes that had befallen Sleptsova, and after a moment's reflection she promised to give us the money we needed. True, she had been saving this money in preparation for a trip to the Paris exhibition of 1890, but freeing a prisoner was more important and so she was prepared to call off her plans.[74]

And so we found ourselves in possession of the thousand rubles we needed! Ostrovskaia and I set out for the procurator's office. This good woman, who led such a tranquil and measured life, did not think, could not have guessed, that she was about to get involved in "politics." The poor woman was so agitated while we were waiting to see the procurator that it pained me to look at her.

When they called my name, we both entered his study. The procurator, sprawled out comfortably in an armchair, looked both of us up and down, from head to foot, and asked in a matter-of-fact, ironic tone of voice: "Well, have you obtained the money?" "And you," he said, turning to my companion, "what is your connection with citizen Sleptsova?" "I'm a relation . . . a relation . . . ," she muttered, shaking all over.

And then our triumphant moment came to pass. Ostrovskaia repaired to a corner and ruffled through the various layers of her skirts, searching for the bundle of money. The procurator, smiling, kept his eyes on her. I tried to help her, but both of our hands were trembling with emotion. Finally, she pulled out the money and placed it on the table. After having counted it carefully, the procurator said: "You can see your Sleptsova—she'll be home shortly."

We left the office. Taking leave of my companion, I flew to Vasil'evskii Island, where Sleptsova lived. It so happened that I had to wait for quite a long time. She returned home later that evening. As it turned out, she had not received a single one of my parcels, books, or letters during her stay in prison.

Incidentally, the reason for Sleptsova's arrest was soon determined. She had an older sister who was an active revolutionary. She was arrested some time before but fled to Switzerland. The police searched a long time for the fugitive and in the end arrested the younger sister.

∗∗∗

I managed to pass in several subjects, but because of all this running back and forth, to and from the chancellery, I had missed one examination. Sleptsova had missed them all; her professors, however, agreed that she could take them after the scheduled date, and so once she was out of prison, Sleptsova set to work studying. In the end, I was scheduled to take my missed examination together with Sleptsova, but I felt so completely worn out that I asked whether I could be allowed to take the exam in the fall. As it turned out, however, this was impossible; our Courses were in their final days. The professor comforted me, promising that the exam would be easy. On the appointed day Sleptsova and I set out together for the university. The professor greeted us very warmly, he showed us his laboratory and conversed with us on various topics, but we could not stop thinking about the trial that awaited us.

Finally, the examination began. I had to answer a question about the flight of birds, but I hadn't read a single word on the subject, and I was very confused, especially since the examination was conducted in the style of a friendly conversation. The professor noticed my discomfort and immediately switched to a different question. In the end, I got a C. Even now it's unpleasant for me to recall this.

XX

Amidst all of my recent efforts and exertions, and with preparing for exams, my spirits had flagged somewhat. My earlier nonchalance and recklessness now disappeared. New thoughts occurred to me, new problems that were not easy to resolve: What would become of me after the Courses? How could I take all of the knowledge that I had acquired here and apply it in the real world? What was I able to do with my life? Whom could I help with what I know, and how? While reading a book, I would often catch myself thinking of something else entirely. A certain sort of uneasiness penetrated my soul and kept me from my studies. I even began to suffer from insomnia.

Finally, I decided to talk about my doubts and to seek the advice of someone who was, to me, an authority. I turned to Professor Miller, whom we all greatly respected, both for the breadth of his thought and for his warmhearted nature. I called on the professor and sat across from him for a long while, silent, gathering my thoughts. He waited patiently, trying to encourage me with a gentle look. Finally, I started speaking, disjointedly and in fits and starts, about everything that was weighing on my soul. After having told him frankly about my doubts, I added that I was thinking about going to Switzerland and enrolling in medical school. Perhaps becoming a doctor might give me the opportunity to fulfill my duty to the people and to humanity at large.

The professor did not interrupt me once. He listened attentively, trying to follow the course of my thoughts to understand them better. After I'd concluded my heartfelt confession, I looked at him. He sat there deep in thought and, after a lengthy pause, began to speak. He took issue with my plans, gently but insistently, especially insofar as a journey abroad would sow discord within the family. "It is possible to live according to one's conscience and be a useful person anywhere and under any conditions," he said. "One needs to rely on one's own instinct, and it will reveal the true path. Each person can do a great deal of good right where he is."

Be that as it may, I heaved a sigh of relief as I left the professor's office. My soul grew calmer. After our conversation, Professor Miller grew dearer to me than ever before. Unfortunately, however, this was to be our final conversation. Orest Fedorovich died soon thereafter, almost right before my very eyes.

It happened like this. A month had passed since our meeting. On my way to the student cafeteria, I saw Professor Miller coming in my direction to say hello. Suddenly he staggered and fell to the ground. Passersby gathered round and helped him to his feet. Gallantly tipping his hat, the professor thanked them for their assistance and continued on his way. When he came up to me, he bowed and I could detect nothing out of the ordinary in his face. But not half an hour had passed before the sorrowful news of Orest Fedorovich's death resounded up and down the Courses, and a whole crowd of us set off for his apartment. It turned out that he had collapsed again outside the entryway of his building and never got up.

Miller's unexpected death fell upon us young students like a thunderbolt, but we were not the only ones affected. Members of the older generation, too, revered this wonderful man, to whom everyone turned for advice and comfort. Not long before, our Orest Fedorovich had delivered a moving speech at Shchedrin's grave, and now, just a few months later, we were burying him alongside Shchedrin.[75] Rest in peace, dear teacher!

We finished our examinations, and the doors of the temple of learning and freedom slammed shut behind us. Like it or not, it was time to step out into the world, to make a fresh start, with new energies and new hopes; after all, without goals and dreams, life is boring and gray. It is necessary always to strive for something greater, even if you only achieve something small—so it seemed to me when I bade farewell to my beloved Petersburg, my beloved courses, my beloved student life. Farewell, youth! Farewell, my carefree life!

With hesitant and halting steps, I was about to embark upon a new life. How would it unfold?

CHAPTER FOUR

Between School and Life

(Vil'na–St. Petersburg, 1890)

I

After completing the Courses, I returned to Vil'na. Once again I spent the summer in Pushkarnia, amid all the beauties of nature. This particular summer passed by uneventfully and left no particular impressions on me. What had happened to my expansiveness, my past enthusiasm for strolls at sunset on moonlit evenings? I had become positively ossified, callous, mired in a spiritual stagnation. Life, it seemed, had ground to a halt. I didn't know what to do, or in what direction to go.

At the end of the summer we went back to town. I felt as if I had nowhere to devote my efforts and energies. I understood that I needed to take up some sort of employment, but I was unable to find anything. In those days we thought little of how work might grant one material independence. We sought only to become independent in our thoughts, in our deeds, and in our choice of actions. Many went into the revolutionary movement in those days, though the movement had still not taken on a mass character. Young people of those times dreamed first and foremost of carrying out cultural and educational work (which I myself undertook after several years of searching, and which remains for me the "meaning of life" to this very day). Social work, as well as purely pedagogical and scholarly endeavors—all fell under the rubric of cultural-enlightenment work.

While in Pushkarnia, I made an attempt to enlighten the working youth at the paper factory. Armed with a couple of pamphlets, I started visiting a young family who worked in the factory and managed to assemble a small reading group. We would read a short little book and then have discussions. This did not last long, however. I was not well suited for such work, and each time I came away unsatisfied, feeling that the young workers were smarter than I and knew more about life. In the end, I switched to teaching them how to read. I was unprepared for revolutionary work; neither, I must say, did I feel particularly drawn toward it.

With our move back to town, my work came to an end, and I sank into a deep depression. I could have loafed around in the bosom of nature, as I used to do during my summer vacations, but after coming back to Vil'na the question "What is to be done?" loomed before me. What to do with all of my energy? And where to direct it? To think that I had prepared myself so eagerly for useful work.

As it turned out, right at this very critical moment, a bookbinding course was established in Vil'na, under the sponsorship of some Polish women who belonged to the local intelligentsia. I seized upon this course as if it were a lifeline, and I resolved to devote myself to the study of handicrafts with extraordinary zeal. My fervor could probably be explained by the fact that I could see no way of putting into practice the abstract knowledge that I had acquired over the past few years. Furthermore, I had always been interested in handicrafts and afterward devoted much time to their study.

Over time, I purchased a great number of tools and instruments required for bookbinding, for trimming edges, and so forth. All of my schoolbooks were tattered, and so I made some beautiful bindings for them, with leather spines and corners. The new bindings turned out marvelously—each book could open easily to any page at all. It's not hard for an intelligent woman to try her hand at handicrafts. I would often say to myself: "An education can prepare one for anything, even housework!"

II

I spent half a year in the bookbinding course. M.M. often came down from Petersburg to stay with us. I felt more and more certain that he was nearer and dearer to me than anyone else I had ever met in my life. Deep within I felt the desire to join my life with that dear man in whose love and noble nature I firmly believed, and whom I loved and respected. I had no doubts whatsoever that our lives were to be closely bound together—I had decided once and for all to marry M.M., and this was all we talked about together. I very much wanted to keep our decision a secret from my parents, to run away with M.M. to Petersburg and get married there, but he was opposed to this and said that he would not want to inflict any grief upon my parents. He resolved to tell them of our decision himself. In the meantime I continued ever more eagerly with my bookbinding and decided to put off our wedding until after the course was completed.

My parents, of course, were delighted that I was not to remain an old maid for the rest of my days. Back then it was thought that a young lady of twenty-four was already past her prime. After dinner, M.M. announced that he was leaving that very night for Petersburg. Having bidden farewell to his circle of friends, he walked up to me, took me by the hand, and gave me a friendly kiss. Turning to my parents he said, with a hint of reproach in his voice: "Believe it or not, this is our first kiss!"

There was much to be done to prepare my trousseau, and my sister found herself with no shortage of things to do. I just wanted something simple, because I did not like fancy things and could not bring myself to wear them. But no matter how much I pleaded, no one listened to me. Mamasha and my sister piled together a whole heap of cloth and material; we had the linens sent out to a convent for the satin embroidery work.

The most important part of the trousseau was the small tea towels. My sister was upset that she wouldn't have time to make more than a dozen. She could not possibly sew enough in such a short period of time, but however could a young woman get married without at least two dozen embroidered tea towels? A solution was found: Mamasha ordered a dozen towels from Moscow, with Russian embroidery work and hand-stitched lace. The other dozen my sister managed to sew herself. Some of the towels had fine lace cross-stitching on both ends. M.M.'s sister gave me such a towel for a present, with young lads and ladies dressed in colorful folk dress and seated in a cross-stitched Russian troika.[1] Such embroidery work took quite a bit of effort!

Tea towels were usually draped over the handle of the samovar when the lady of the house poured the tea. The teacups would be washed right at the table in a basin and thoroughly dried with the towels. This ritual took place three times a day: in the morning, in the afternoon after lunch, and right before supper. I must confess that even now I still miss those afternoons and evenings spent in front of the samovar, though I haven't laid eyes on that tea set since 1911.

I did not concern myself with the hustle and bustle surrounding my bridal linens. It was even worse with respect to the dresses and overcoat, since I had to try those on. Between the dresses and the bonnets and the outfits, there were eighteen pieces all together! They were typical for the fashions of those days, and I can still remember some of them: a black morning coat, which I wore only once, made out of a thick soft silk that fit tightly around the waist (it had a bodice made out of whalebone and a pointed collar that resembled that of Mary, Queen of Scots). There was a little blue woolen outfit, too; the dress was embroidered with a light blue border, and the vest was lined with light blue silk. This was a modest suit, but fun and stylish, and I wore it often. Most of the dresses that went into my trousseau, however, I never even wore. The peignoir was especially comical; it was made of a bright red taffeta with long sleeves that fell almost to the ground and a cream-colored lace inset embroidered in gold. With it came a set of matching oriental slippers in the Caucasus style, made of soft red leather and embroidered with the same gold stitching. And to think that this sort of toilette was deemed appropriate for a young woman who had just graduated from the Bestuzhev Courses, who had democratic views and aspired to physical labor!

Among the many coats that were made for me, a splendidly thick fur coat stood out. In those days women wore capes resembling a broad pelerine, and ladies who were not very tall looked almost spherical in them. My cape was lined with fluffy yellow fox fur; the top was made out of thin plush silk, the color of seawater, and the collar was made out of black vixen. This magnificent outfit might have been worn by the most elegant lady pulling up to the theater in a horse-drawn carriage, but it was completely unsuited for someone who needed to wait long hours in line at the box office to purchase gallery seats. I never did wear the fur coat. In fact, five years afterward I unstitched the lining, sold the fur for a pittance, and used the plush to upholster the armchairs in our living room. I did wear, however, another coat that was made from an expensive dark red velvet stuffed with down, lined with black silk, and with a tiny damask collar that fit tightly around the neck. It was sewn in Petersburg by a good tailor, and despite its elegance it had a look of modesty about it. At first I was shy about wearing it, but in time I grew used to it, and even quite fond of it, and wore it for a long time to come. Besides these two coats, I also had a cloth coat lined with white fur and a smallish collar, a matching hat, and a muff made out of Persian lamb. This coat corresponded exactly to my station in life and my internal character, if I may say so. It served me faithfully for more than ten years. Generally speaking, I have dressed in the same sort of style throughout my entire life. Friends told me that I had my own look.

III

Not long before the wedding, my sister and I left for Petersburg to rent and furnish a room. Several weeks before I had written to M.M. concerning our arrival, but he kept telling us not to hurry. I got tired of this, and so we set out for the capital. M.M. met us at the station with a dejected look on his face. The fact of the matter was that all this time he had been bustling about to obtain residency rights for me and had still not received official permission.[2] I simply could not believe that I did not have the right to spend a couple of days in the very same city where I had lived so happily for four whole years. However, there was nothing to be done. M.M. put us up at a three-star hotel on Sadovaia Street, though he himself stayed in his private apartment in the Five Corners neighborhood. It was possible to stay in this particular hotel for a few nights without official registration. I felt like a real nobody in this grand hotel. Nevertheless, my sister and I began to search about for an apartment. M.M. gave me complete freedom, but, due to my lack of experience in this matter, I made quite a few blunders.

For one, it never even occurred to me that a doctor just beginning his profession ought to live close by his office. I fell in love with an apartment that was located not far from my beloved Mariinskii Theater; the famous opera singer Koriakin had lived here for eleven years, and this was reason enough for me to stop my search. It seemed as if echoes of all the arias I loved so well were coming from the very walls themselves!

The apartment had seven rooms, but, as we soon realized, it was far too expensive for us. It was strange to think that I, who had grown up in a merchant family, placed no importance whatsoever on material considerations. We bought everything for the apartment at the Apraksin market—which meant that it was not very expensive. My parents gave me some money to buy furniture, and I spent a whole third of it on a Schröder grand piano.[3]

We spent two weeks in Petersburg. We ran about from store to store in the afternoons, and in the evenings we went to the theater. In our spare time, my sister sewed little cushions for me; she considered these to be of the utmost necessity in furnishing a young couple's home and managed to sew a half dozen of them.

When we returned from Petersburg, the preparations began for the wedding. I had already successfully completed my bookbinding courses, and so, with no impediments, the wedding was set for March 11. M.M. arrived a week before the ceremony.

At this point, I was able to become better acquainted with M.M.'s parents and his family situation. His father was a contractor. Contractors were a special type, unlike ordinary merchants. In those days, merchants had their own distinct qualities, their own ethos. While a merchant worked from one day to the next without rest, a contractor lived, as the saying goes, "as the wind blows." In the course of a year or two he might grow wealthy, and then once again find himself stalled at sea, adrift, waiting for the weather to turn, living lightly off his easily earned moneys. In any event, this was the impression I had when I compared my merchant parents with M.M.'s.

My father-in-law had made his fortune during the Russo-Turkish war, and since that time was able to support two families, his and his brother's.[4] M.M.'s father lived in his own house, which was always full of people: guests were constantly coming by for dinner, and many of them played cards there day and night. The master of the house was a fellow who liked to live life on a grand scale. He looked the part of a wealthy Russian merchant: he had fair hair, thick and straight, that hung in ringlets round his head; he had strong facial features and a broad beard, soft and long. He was an intelligent and good-hearted man—everyone around him lived at his expense. He was not averse to having a drink and kept a decent supply of wine and other alcoholic beverages in his cellar.

He loved to tell friends and family the story of how his parents had married him off. They had arranged the match while he was still going to heder, and he never saw the bride until the day of the wedding. Someone spread the rumor that the bride was a hunchback, and his friends from heder made quite a few jokes at the expense of the poor groom-to-be. As soon as he arrived in the little town where the bride lived and where the wedding was to be held, he spied on his future father-in-law's three daughters from far off and made sure that all their backs were straight. On the day of the wedding he sat in his room from morning to night and shot marbles with his friends. Finally, they dressed him and stood him beneath the wedding canopy, and only then did he first lay eyes on his future lifelong companion, who would subsequently bear him twelve children.

IV

M.M.'s parents maintained absolutely no semblance of order in the house. It seemed as if there were no one to enforce the rules. Guests who came to the house stayed as long as they saw fit and apparently felt more comfortable here than they did in their own homes. One female relation who came to visit felt so at home that she stayed several years. In time, M.M.'s parents married her off and gave her a dowry.

My mother-in-law's main task, it seemed, was to cook and bake as much as possible. She specialized in making all sorts of preserves and cookies, such as *teiglach* and *eingemachts*.[5] She was especially famous for her skill in fattening up the chickens and geese they kept. Truth be told, I couldn't even begin to list all of my mother-in-law's specialties.

The furnishings in M.M.'s home were not to my liking. When we were engaged, we each agreed to talk to our parents about not giving us any wedding presents. I was especially worried that my mother-in-law might give me diamond jewelry, which was practically mandatory in bourgeois circles. And sure enough, after we'd finished dinner one evening, and in front of M.M.'s entire family, his mother laid before me an open case containing a brooch with three large diamonds. I was amazed. Everyone fell silent and stared at my reddened face.

I could not refrain from casting a furious glance at M.M., who sat beside me. I did not bother touching the case and did not utter one word of thanks. A simple soul, M.M.'s mother decided that I simply did not like the diamonds and was very confused. M.M. attempted to smooth over the incident—he quickly pocketed the case, and that was the end of the affair.

In reality, M.M. could not be blamed. He had discussed the matter with his parents, but they concluded that they simply could not make do without the diamonds, even though their financial situation was in sharp decline at the time. That same day, M.M. gave the case with the diamond brooch to my sister, and she held on to it for twelve years. At the time I swore to her that I would never put on the jewelry—and I kept my word. In fact, only once in that whole time did my diamonds ever see the light of day. Once, when I was visiting my sister in Vil'na, I went with her to a wedding. My sister simply could not come to terms with the fact that I would never wear the diamonds, and when she took out her own brooch, she took out mine as well, begging me to wear it. I remained steadfast. And then, during the wedding, when we were sitting at the dining table, my sister noticed, with horror, that I wasn't wearing the brooch—it was still lying atop the vanity. My brother-in-law had to hurry home and hide the ill-favored diamonds. They remained with my sister for another five or six years. They were finally taken out at my request, but for an entirely different purpose.[6]

V

Our wedding date was set for Tuesday, March 11. Weddings, of course, are usually arranged for a "lucky day"—Tuesday. After all, how could such a day not bring good fortune to the couple![7]

At home, we had endless conversations about wedding procedures. My parents considered that the situation called for it. My sister's wedding, after all, had been a modest one and was held in the town of Landvarov, outside of Vil'na. But in the time between my sister's wedding and my own, our parents had grown wealthier: Papasha was not only a merchant of the first guild, but now also a factory owner.[8] On account of the family's increased wealth, my dowry, trousseau, and wedding ceremony were to be much more impressive than my sister's. My sister had only received four thousand rubles, but I was given ten thousand. When the time came for our youngest sister's wedding, our parents gave Idochka forty thousand rubles for her dowry.[9]

In those days we had no social clubs or restaurants in town. But after a long search for a location that would be large enough, we finally found an unlet apartment that consisted of several spacious rooms. With her ample talents, Mamasha furnished the apartment and decorated it with curtains, rugs, and flowers, in an attempt to give the place a "lived-in" look. For the actual ceremony, some sort of structure resembling a throne, covered with a carpet and decorated with plants and flowers, was hoisted atop the dais.[10] The long path that led through all the rooms was covered with a long and beautiful carpet, with potted myrtles on either side. Lots of time and energy was spent on the menu for the wedding feast. Besides the traditional fish and poultry, there were also some curious and exotic dishes. The wine was also expensive, especially for the table where the guests of honor were seated; this was done so that no one might say the wedding organizers were stingy with the wine. Each table was piled high with mounds of fruit and some of the choicest sweets.

The wedding promised to be quite splendid, and the entire town grew eager with anticipation. The shops and stores did a brisk trade. The tailors paid overtime to their workers, who labored day and night. Business was especially lively in the jewelry shops, since everyone who was planning to attend the wedding considered it their duty to give a present. Those guests who had business connections with the Paperna factory were especially eager to show off their generosity.

Before the wedding our entire living room was filled with vases and various ornaments. For some reason we received a great number of sugar basins as gifts. I especially remember one silver and gilded sugar basin, which was given to us by the contractor who supplied wood to the factory; his initials (I. P.) and mine (A. P.) were engraved on the basin in French script. This sugar basin irritated me because of how closely our initials resembled each other. M.M. laughed at me and nicknamed the sugar basin: "To Ap from Ip." Some years later, I got rid of the sugar basin: it suffered the same fate as my diamonds.

I liked to receive presents only from people who were near and dear to me. As I recall, the only wedding present that truly made me happy was given to me by my brother: a set of the complete works of Saltykov-Shchedrin. My brother knew that I simply adored this author.

VI

March 11 finally came. I must confess that in the end the festive mood caught hold of me as well. Before the wedding, I distanced myself from all the preparations and all the commotion, as if I had nothing to do with any of it. On the day of the wedding, however, I became the center of everyone's attention. My sister was particularly frenzied and bustled all about me.

All the commotion was to make certain that all the clothes and trimmings needed for the wedding were carefully prepared ahead of time and carefully laid out. The wedding dress itself was made out of the most expensive damask silk and had a long train that measured about 1.5 *arshins*.[11] A matching sortie de bal was sewn for the dress, made from the same type of silk, lined with down, and trimmed with white fur. Everything was prepared most magnificently, and the tailor who sewed my entire wardrobe deserves full credit. Apart from my dress, there were a whole host of matching accessories: white satin shoes, white silk stockings (at that time silk stockings were very difficult to obtain and were worn only on the most special occasions), a long veil made of silk tulle that reached to the very bottom of the dress (this was spread out atop a couple of chairs so it would not wrinkle), and most important of all, a fan, which was supposed to be given to the bride by the groom. The bride needed to have a fan, made out of expensive ostrich feathers, that matched her dress. My sister was quite nervous about the fan and only calmed down once it arrived. To tell the truth, the fan was not made out of ostrich feathers at all, but from ivory; it was quite old, with remarkable needlework.

The handkerchief also played an important role in the wedding attire: it simply had to be stitched by a genuine Viennese lace maker. And for the pièce de résistance, the groom was supposed to send a bouquet of magnificent white roses, tied together with a wide moiré ribbon.

At the break of dawn on the day of the wedding, Mamasha was scurrying about, making arrangements at the apartment where the wedding was to take place. My sister stayed at home so that she could make sure everyone in the family was dressed properly. Although by that time my sister lived in her own home, she and her children got dressed at our place. Without my sister I wouldn't have been able to manage, especially at such an important moment in my life. M.M. spent about an hour with us that day and then left so that we could start our ritual preparations. The wedding ceremony was scheduled for four o'clock, so that we would be able to leave for Petersburg on the eleven o'clock train.

In addition to my family, a few of the girls from my parents' store were scurrying about, only adding to the general noise and confusion. One of the seamstresses was called in from the dress shop; she was there to help me put on the wedding dress and the veil. For the veil to sit properly on my head, I needed to have my hair worn up and styled just so; there was a hairdresser on hand to fix things in the proper fashion.

Never once in my life—not before and not after the wedding—have I gone to a salon to get my hair styled, and besides, I never did like to change my appearance. On any other occasion, I would have protested vigorously against any attempt to change my hairstyle, but on this day, I did not want to argue. My hair was very thick and long, but the stylist was given carte blanche, and, with the help of an incredible number of hairpins of various shapes and sizes, a real Eiffel Tower was erected atop my head.

From this moment forth, my individuality vanished—I felt confined and embarrassed by this enormous hairdo and this heavy dress with a long train that restricted my movement. The long, embroidered veil constrained me as well, tangling up everybody and everything around me like a cobweb. All of these things combined gave me a rather uncertain and hesitant look. Perhaps this is how things are supposed to be for a bride, but I received no pleasure from any of it. Only the feeling that this wasn't the real me helped me perform the role that others expected me to play. It made no difference to me how I looked. I made a solemn promise to myself that as soon as the wedding ceremony was over, I would take off the veil and comb my hair the way I always did.

When I appeared before my family all dressed up, everyone gasped with delight. I took one look at myself in the mirror but could not bear a second glance. This was not me in the mirror, but rather an image of what a bride was supposed to look like. I did not like my bridal attire in the least, especially not the veil, which was not well suited to my face. With a bouquet of roses in one hand, and the fan and handkerchief in the other, I waited in agonized anticipation.

Finally, Papasha came for me, all pale and nervous. A magnificent white fur-collared coat was thrown over my veil, and, escorted by Papasha, my sister, and a whole entourage, we set out for the covered carriage. My dress and I took up both of the front seats, so Papasha and my sister sat opposite me. A rug was laid on the steps of the carriage so that I wouldn't dirty my white satin shoes.

When we arrived, Father took me by the arm and walked me past a long row of guests, who stood on either side of the carpet that ran through all three rooms of the apartment, leading all the way to the dais. Children ran in front of me, throwing flowers at my feet.

A person feels a bit foolish when all eyes are fixed upon her. I felt painfully ill at ease, and the whole time I thought only of how I wanted this whole spectacle to come to an end. I simply was not suited to play such a role!

Every minute seemed like an eternity to me. Finally, I was asked to take a seat; my dear friends sat on either side of me. The wedding canopy was brought out and placed in the center of the hall. Someone came to me—I think it was my sister and her husband—took me by the hand, and escorted me under the canopy. Another couple escorted M.M. and stood him next to me. From this moment on, I looked at no one but M.M. The entire wedding ceremony seemed like a dream to me. I waited impatiently for it to be over.

After the ceremony had finished, everyone gathered round the dinner table. The meal, which would ordinarily last for no longer than half an hour, dragged on for more than three. It was already nearly ten o'clock in the evening, and it was time for the guests to go home so that we would have time to change our clothes before our departure. But no one had even touched the sweets that were arranged on special tables, nobody had started dancing yet, and the guests had not even had time to admire to their hearts' content the pretty young ladies, of whom Vil'na had its fair share in those days. And so a group of young people requested—or, more accurately, demanded—that we postpone our departure until the following morning.

The older guests agreed with our young friends. My sister and parents also started pleading that we postpone the departure. I was under pressure from all sides. But I held my ground: "No way!"

Perhaps if my sister had thought to whisper to me that I could come back to my very own room after the wedding, it's possible that I might have yielded. But it didn't turn out that way, and I remained steadfast. Slightly offended, the guests began to take their leave. My family, distressed by my stubbornness, hurried home so that they would have time to change clothes and escort us to the train station.

At the station many guests showed up with flowers to bid us farewell. Even as we were leaving, I had the presence of mind to bring with me all the bookbinding tools I'd need.

Notes

Introduction

1. Simon Dubnow (1860–1941) was a prominent Russian Jewish historian, publicist, and political thinker. Born in Mstislavl in the Pale of Settlement, Dubnow founded the Jewish Historical-Ethnographic Society, edited *Jewish Encyclopedia*, and championed cultural autonomy and civil rights for Jews and other nationalities in the Russian Empire.

Dubnow is best known for authoring *World History of the Jewish People*, which appeared in ten volumes, and for his autobiography, *The Book of Life: Reminiscences and Reflections*, published in three volumes. Dubnow was murdered by the Nazis in Riga.

2. A. P. Vygodskaia, *Istoriia odnoi zhizni: Vospominaniia* (Riga: Dzīve un kultūra, 1938).

3. Review of *Istoriia odnoi zhizni* by F. Stogov in *Segodnia* (Riga), March 11, 1939. Dubnow's daughter wrote in her memoirs that Vygodskaia's autobiography was also reviewed by the celebrated Russian historian and liberal politician Pavel Miliukov in the émigré periodical *Russkie zapiski* (Paris–Shanghai). Vygodskaia's memoir does appear in a list of books received for review in the June 18, 1939, issue of *Russkie zapiski*, but we have not been able to locate a review by Miliukov. See Sofiia Dubnova-Erlikh, *Khleb i matsa: Vospominaniia* (St. Petersburg: Maksima, 1994), 225.

4. For a recent analysis of love and marriage in *The Story of a Life*, see Birte Kohtz, "Ausgesetz auf den Bergen des Herzens? Liebe und Ehseschliessung in der Autobiographie Anna Pavlovna Vygodskajas," in *Vom Wir zum Ich: Individuum and Autobiographik im Zarenreich*, ed. Julia Herzberg and Christoph Schmidt (Köln: Böhlau Verlag, 2007), 217–41.

5. For an informative introduction to women's autobiographies in Tsarist Russia, see Toby W. Clyman and Judith Vowles, eds., *Russia through Women's Eyes: Autobiographies from Tsarist Russia* (New Haven: Yale University Press, 1996), 1–46. For the most extensive examination of Jewish autobiography in Eastern Europe, see Marcus Moseley, *Being for Myself Alone: Origins of Jewish Autobiography* (Stanford: Stanford University Press, 2006).

6. See, for example, Hinde Bergner, *On a Long Winter's Night: Memoirs of a Jewish Family in a Galician Township, 1870–1900*, ed. and trans. Justin Cammy (Cambridge: Harvard University Press, 2005); Puah Rakovska, *My Life as a Radical Jewish Woman: Memoirs of a Zionist Feminist in Poland*, ed. and trans. Paula E. Hyman (Bloomington: Indiana University Press, 2001); and Pauline Wengeroff, *Memoirs of a Grandmother: Scenes from the Cultural History of the Jews of Russia in the Nineteenth Century*, vol. 1, ed. and trans. Shulamit S. Magnus (Stanford: Stanford University Press, 2010). Vygodskaia's memoir does not appear in the most complete bibliography of East European Jewish memoirs. Karen Auerbach, "Bibliography: Jewish Women in Eastern Europe," *Polin* 18 (2005): 273–88.

7. On the participation of Jews in Russia's civil society, see Benjamin Nathans, *Beyond the Pale: The Jewish Encounter with Late Imperial Russia* (Berkeley: University of California Press, 2002); Yvonne Kleinmann, *Neue Orte—neue Menschen: Jüdisches Leben in St. Petersburg und Moskau* (Göttingen: Vandenhoeck and Ruprecht, 2006); and Jeffrey Veidlinger, *Jewish Public Culture in the Late Russian Empire* (Bloomington: Indiana University Press, 2009). For a discussion of the imperial Russian context, see Joseph Bradley, *Voluntary Associations in Tsarist Russia: Science, Patriotism, and Civil Society* (Cambridge: Harvard University Press, 2009).

8. For an excellent discussion of the historiography of Jewish women in Eastern Europe, see ChaeRan Freeze and Paula Hyman, "Introduction: A Historiographical Survey," *Polin* 18 (2005): 3–24.

9. For a broad overview of the fragmentary archive and the problem of narration of (feminist) biography, see Marilyn Booth and Antoinette Burton, "Editors' Note: Critical Feminist Biography," *Journal of Women's History* 21, no. 3 (2009): 7–8. See also Burton, *Dwelling in the Archive: Women Writing House, Home, and History in Late Colonial India* (Oxford: Oxford University Press, 2003); and Michelle Perrot, ed., *A History of Private Life: From the Fires of Revolution to the Great War*, vol. 4, trans. Arthur Goldhammer (Cambridge: Belknap Press of Harvard University Press, 1990), 3–4.

10. On the challenges of narrating and analyzing women's experiences, see Nupur Chaudhuri, Sherry J. Katz, and Mary Elizabeth Perry, eds., *Contesting Archives: Finding Women in the Sources* (Urbana: University of Illinois Press, 2010).

11. For a recent critical assessment of the autobiographical genre in Jewish studies, see Michael Stanislawski, *Autobiographical Jews: Essays in Jewish Self-Fashioning* (Seattle: University of Washington Press, 2004). Simon Dubnow entrusted his daughter with the editing and revision of Vygodskaia's lengthy manuscript prior to publication. "It was clear," Dubnova-Erlikh recalled, "that the raw material still needed to be transformed into a book," a task that required several months' work and much assurance to Vygodskaia that the changes made would be cosmetic and not affect the content. See Dubnova-Erlikh, *Khleb i matsa*, 225. Vygodskaia was not the only memoirist who asked for editorial assistance. The artist David Kassel, for example, edited Yekhezkel Kotik's memoirs, *Mayne zikhroynes*. According to the historian David Assaf, editorial assistance was an "accepted practice," and "even experienced authors were not exempt from the

need for editorial intervention." See Yekhezkel Kotik, *Journey to a Nineteenth-Century Shtetl: The Memoirs of Yekhezkel Kotik*, ed. David Assaf (Detroit: Wayne State University Press, 2002), 57.

12. For the most authoritative account of the emergence of Jewish communities outside the boundaries of the Pale of Settlement, see Nathans, *Beyond the Pale.* For a discussion of the politics of Jewish movement and residence, see Eugene M. Avrutin, *Jews and the Imperial State: Identification Politics in Tsarist Russia* (Ithaca: Cornell University Press, 2010), 86–115.

13. On the social and economic development of Bobruisk, see Yehuda Slutsky, ed., *Bobroysk: Yizker-bukh far Bobroysker kehileh un umgegnt* (Tel Aviv: Tarbut ve-hinukh, 1967), 124–32; and *Bobruisk: Istoriko-ekonomichesii ocherk,* 2nd ed. (Minsk: Belarus, 1970), 5–19.

14. "Bobruisk," in *Evreiskaia entsiklopediia: Svod znanii o evreistve i ego kul'ture v proshlom i nastoiashchem,* 16 vols. (Moscow: Terra, 1991), 4: 688.

15. On the social origins of Hasidism, see Moshe Rosman, *Founder of Hasidism: A Quest for the Historical Ba'al Shem Tov* (Berkeley: University of California Press, 1996); and Glenn Dynner, *Men of Silk: The Hasidic Conquest of Polish Jewish Society* (Oxford: Oxford University Press, 2006). On the religious wars, see Mordecai Wilensky, "Hasidic-Mitnaggedic Polemics in the Jewish Communities of Eastern Europe: The Hostile Phase," in *Essential Papers on Hasidism,* ed. Gershon D. Hundert (New York: New York University Press, 1991), 224–74.

16. As quoted in *Bobruisk,* 18.

17. Slutsky, ed., *Bobroysk,* 125–26.

18. On the cultural and social development of urban communities in the western borderlands, see Rebecca Kobrin, *Jewish Bialystok and Its Diaspora* (Bloomington: Indiana University Press, 2010), 19–55; Veidlinger, *Jewish Public Culture in the Late Russian Empire*; and Natan M. Meir, *Kiev, Jewish Metropolis: A History, 1859–1914* (Bloomington: Indiana University Press, 2010).

19. On the Paperna family, see Avraam I. Paperna's autobiographical reflections, "Vospominaniia: Detstvo i iunost'," *Perezhitoe* 3 (1911): 264–364.

20. For a discussion of social and religious change in Germany, see Steven M. Lowenstein, *The Berlin Jewish Community: Enlightenment, Family, and Crisis, 1770–1830* (New York: Oxford University Press, 1994), and "The Beginnings of Integration, 1780–1870," in *Jewish Daily Life in Germany, 1618–1945,* ed. Marion A. Kaplan (Oxford: Oxford University Press, 2005), 93–171.

21. Paperna, "Vospominaniia," 285–86.

22. Paperna recalled that only around a dozen *maskilim* (followers of the Jewish Enlightenment) had resided in Bobruisk when his family relocated to the town. "Vospominaniia," 361.

23. On Jews and the gold-mining industry in Siberia, see L. V. Kal'mina, *Evreiskie obshchiny vostochnoi Sibiri (seredina xix v.–fevral' 1917 goda)* (Ulan-ude: Izdatel'sko-poligraficheskoi kompleks VSGAKI, 2003), 145–51. On the acculturation of Jews in Siberia, see Viktoriia Romanova, *Vlast' i evrei na Dal'nem Vostoke Rossii: Istoriia vzaimootnoshenii (vtoraia polovina xix v.–20-e gody xx v.)* (Krasnoiarsk: Klaretianum, 2001), 27.

24. For the most exhaustive treatment of the seminaries, see Verena Dohrn, *Jüdische Eliten im Russischen Reich: Aufklärung und Integration im 19 Jahrhundert* (Köln: Böhlau, 2008), 124–93. See also Michael Stanislawski, *Tsar Nicholas I and the Jews: The Transformation of Jewish Society in Russia, 1825–1855* (Philadelphia: Jewish Publication Society of America, 1983), 97–109.

25. On gender differences in the educational system in the East European Jewish community, see Iris Parush, *Reading Jewish Women: Marginality and Modernization in Nineteenth-Century Eastern European Jewish Society*, trans. Saadya Sternberg (Waltham, MA: Brandeis University Press, 2004), 57–70; and Shaul Stampfer, "Gender Differentiation and Education of the Jewish Woman in Nineteenth-Century Eastern Europe," *Polin* 7 (1992): 63–87. A firsthand account is provided in Ben-Zion Gold, *The Life of Jews in Poland before the Holocaust: A Memoir* (Lincoln: University of Nebraska Press, 2007).

26. On Russification policies, see Theodore R. Weeks, *Nation and State in Late Imperial Russia: Nationalism and Russification on the Western Frontier, 1863–1914* (DeKalb: Northern Illinois University Press, 1996); and Andreas Kappeler, *The Russian Empire: A Multi-Ethnic History*, trans. Alfred Clayton (London: Longman, 2001). See also Darius Staliunas, *Making Russians: Meaning and Practice of Russification in Lithuania and Belarus* (Amsterdam: Radopi, 2007).

27. For a recent discussion of archival documentation and the problem of Jewish neighborly relations in the Russian Empire, see Eugene M. Avrutin, "Jewish Neighbourly Relations and Imperial Russian Legal Culture," *Journal of Modern Jewish Studies* 9, no. 1 (2010): 1–16. On the importance of memoirs and other autobiographical sources for analyzing Jewish neighborly relations, see Marion Kaplan, "Friendship on the Margins: Jewish Social Relations in Imperial Germany," *Central European History* 34, no. 4 (2001): 471–501.

28. As quoted in Parush, *Reading Jewish Women*, 31. On the politics of language in the era of the Great Reforms, see John D. Klier, *Imperial Russia's Jewish Question, 1855–1881* (Cambridge: Cambridge University Press, 1995), 145–262; and Harriet Murav, *Identity Theft: The Jew in Imperial Russia and the Case of Avraam Uri Kovner* (Stanford: Stanford University Press, 2003), 60–82.

29. Parush, *Reading Jewish Women*, 83–84. On the debates in the press, see Eliyana R. Adler, "Women's Education in the Pages of the Russian Jewish Press," *Polin* 18 (2005): 121–32.

30. For a short history of Vil'na, see Mordechai Zalkin, "Vilnius," in *YIVO Encyclopedia of Jews in Eastern Europe*, ed. Gershon David Hundert, 2 vols. (New Haven: Yale University Press, 2008), 2:1970–77.

31. Parush, *Reading Jewish Women*; and Shulamit S. Magnus, "Introduction," in *Memoirs of a Grandmother*, 16, 52–57. For a comprehensive analysis of the gendered division of secularization in Jewish communities, see Paula E. Hyman, *Gender and Assimilation in Modern Jewish History: The Roles and Representation of Women* (Seattle: University of Washington Press, 1995), 50–92.

32. Barbara Alpern Engel, *Women in Russia, 1700–2000* (Cambridge: Cambridge University Press, 2004), 71–80.

33. On the education of Jewish women in the Russian Empire, see Nathans, *Beyond the Pale*, 222–24; Eliyana R. Adler, *In Her Hands: The Education of Jewish Girls in Tsarist Russia* (Detroit: Wayne State University Press, 2010); and Carole B. Balin, "The Call to Serve: Jewish Women Students in Russia, 1872–1887," *Polin* 18 (2005): 133–52. On the role of philanthropic institutions, especially the Society for the Promotion of Enlightenment, for sponsoring schools for both girls and boys, see Brian Horowitz, *Jewish Philanthropy and Enlightenment in Late-Tsarist Russia* (Seattle: University of Washington Press, 2009).

34. For an analysis of the gendered dimensions of mobility in the Russian Empire, see V. A. Veremenko, "'Litso s vidom na zhitel'stvo': Gender'nyi aspekt pasportnoi sistemy Rossii kontsa XIX–nachala XX vv.," *Adam & Eva: Al'manakh gendernoi istorii* 7 (2004): 201–42; and Barbara Alpern Engel, *Breaking the Ties That Bound: The Politics of Marital Strife in Late Imperial Russia* (Ithaca: Cornell University Press, 2011), 16–18, 260.

35. Conversion to Russian Orthodoxy, Catholicism, or Protestantism awarded Jews automatic residence privileges beyond the Pale. For an excellent study of gender and conversion, see ChaeRan Freeze, "When Chava Left Home: Gender, Conversion, and the Jewish Family in Tsarist Russia," *Polin* 18 (2005): 153–88. In her memoirs, Puah Rakovska describes the challenges of traveling to St. Petersburg without her husband's permission. See *My Life as a Radical Jewish Woman*, 38. For a discussion of fictitious marriages, see Engel, *Women in Russia*, 72–74.

36. On the expulsions of Jews from St. Petersburg, see Nathans, *Beyond the Pale*, 99–100.

37. Ibid., 218, 224. On Jewish population statistics, see Kappeler, *Russian Empire*, 397–99.

38. See Cynthia H. Whittaker, "The Women's Movement during the Reign of Alexander II: A Case Study in Russian Liberalism," *Journal of Modern History* 48, no. 2, suppl. (June 1976): 35–69; Richard Stites, *The Women's Liberation Movement in Russia: Feminism, Nihilism, and Bolshevism, 1860–1930* (Princeton: Princeton University Press, 1978), 50–56; Ruth A. Dudgeon, "The Forgotten Minority: Women Students in Imperial Russia, 1872–1917," *Russian History* 9 (1982): 1–26; and Engel, *Women in Russia*, 108–15.

39. Christine Johanson, *Women's Struggle for Higher Education in Russia, 1855–1900* (Kingston, ON: McGill-Queen's University Press, 1987), 72–76; Whittaker, "Women's Movement," 57–58; Stites, *Women's Liberation Movement*, 82–83; and S. N. Valk, ed., *Sankt-Peterburgskie vysshie zhenskie (Bestuzhevskie) kursy, 1878–1918: Sbornik statei* (Leningrad: Izdatel'stvo Leningradskogo universiteta, 1973).

40. On the popularity of scientific studies among Russian women students, see Barbara Alpern Engel, "Women Medical Students in Russia, 1872–1882: Reformers or Rebels?" *Journal of Social History* 12 (1979): 394–414; and Dmitri Gouzévitch and Irina Gouzévitch, "The Difficult Challenges of No Man's Land, or the Russian Road to the Professionalization of Women's Engineering (1850–1920)," *Quaderns d'Història de l'Enginyeria* 4 (2000): 133–83.

41. Christine Ruane, *Gender, Class, and the Professionalization of Russian City Teachers, 1860–1914* (Pittsburgh: University of Pittsburgh Press, 1994), 33.

42. Susan K. Morrisey, *Heralds of Revolution: Russian Students and the Mythologies of Radicalism* (Oxford: Oxford University Press, 1998), 23. On *studenchestvo* at the Bestuzhev Courses, see Samuel D. Kassow, *Students, Professors, and the State in Tsarist Russia* (Berkeley: University of California Press, 1989), 87.

43. Stites, *Women's Liberation Movement*, 172. On the difficult material conditions of female students, see Dudgeon, "Forgotten Minority," 22–23; and Engel, *Women in Russia*, 111.

44. Stites, *Women's Liberation Movement*, 168.

45. Whittaker, "Women's Movement," 62.

46. Dudgeon, "Forgotten Minority," 7–8.

47. Vera Figner, *Memoirs of a Revolutionist* (DeKalb: Northern Illinois University Press, 1991), 23.

48. Similar sentiments are expressed in the posthumously published diaries of Elizaveta D'iakonova, who graduated from the Bestuzhev Courses in 1899, a decade after Vygodskaia. See *Dnevnik Elizavety D'iakonovoi, Literaturnye etiudy-stat'i* (St. Petersburg: Kushnerov, 1905). Recent scholarship suggests such idealistic sentiments were widespread among educated Russian professionals. See Harley D. Balzer, "Introduction," in *Russia's Missing Middle Class: The Professions in Russian History*, ed. Harley D. Balzer (Armonk, NY: M. E. Sharpe, 1996), 3–38. Our thanks to Barbara Alpern Engel for her insights into this question.

49. On mass consumerism and leisure-time activities, see Christine Ruane, *The Empire's New Clothes: A History of the Russian Fashion Industry, 1700–1917* (New Haven: Yale University Press, 2009); and Louise McReynolds, *Russia at Play: Leisure Activities at the End of the Tsarist Era* (Ithaca: Cornell University Press, 2002). On the musical world, see James Loeffler, *The Most Musical Nation: Jews and Culture in the Late Russian Empire* (New Haven: Yale University Press, 2010).

50. A short biographical entry on Mikhail Markovich Vygodskii appears in Iu. I. Rafes, *Evreiskii vrach v vostochnoi Evrope. Vil'no: Stranitsy istorii XIX vek–1943 g.* (New York: Gelany, 2006), 15.

51. On marriage and sexuality, see ChaeRan Freeze, *Jewish Marriage and Divorce in Imperial Russia* (Waltham: Brandeis University Press, 2002).

52. This paragraph draws on Regina Weinreich's short biographical sketch of Anna Vygodskaia's life. See Kh. Sh. Kazdan, ed., *Lerer-yizker-bukh* (New York: Marstin Press, 1954), 144–45.

53. The Sofia M. Gurevitch Gymnasium archive, which contains petitions and reports from Sofia Gurevitch to the Ministry of Education, minutes of meetings, and other official records, is preserved at the Institute for Jewish Research (YIVO), RG 51. The documents are not paginated. Anna Vygodskaia's name and signature appear on several of the papers. In 1918, the Gurevitch Gymnasium adopted a Yiddishist secular approach to education.

54. Rita Kramer, *Maria Montessori: A Biography* (New York: G. P. Putnam's Sons, 1976), 246.

55. Iu. I. Fausek, *Detskii sad Montessori. Opyty i nabliudeniia v techenie semiletnei raboty v detskikh sadakh po sisteme Montessori* (Berlin: Izdatel'stvo Z. I. Grzhebina, 1923).

56. A. P. Vygodskaia, *K materiam* (Novgorod: Tipografiia Gubsoiuza, 1920), 3.

57. Ibid., 3, 6–7.

58. On the social dislocations produced by the civil war, see Daniel R. Brower, "'The City in Danger': The Civil War and the Russian Urban Population," in *Party, State, and Society in the Russian Civil War: Explorations in Social History*, ed. Diane P. Koenker, William G. Rosenberg, and Ronald Grigor Suny (Bloomington: Indiana University Press, 1989), 58–80.

59. A. P. Vygodskaia, "Postanovka gramoty v detskom sadu," *Narodnoe prosveshchenie*, no. 6–7 (1919): 60.

60. Vera Semenova, "90 let Montessori-pedagogike v Rossii," *Doshkol'noe obrazovanie*, no. 10/226 (2008), http://dob.1september.ru/article.php?ID=200801009. On educational policy in the new Soviet state, see Larry E. Holmes, *The Kremlin and the Schoolhouse: Reforming Education in Soviet Russia, 1917–1931* (Bloomington: Indiana University Press, 1991).

61. On interwar Poland, see Ezra Mendelsohn, *The Jews of East Central Europe between the World Wars* (Bloomington: Indiana University Press, 1983), 11–83.

62. "Der Tsentraler Bildungs-Komitet in Vilne," in *Yidishe Vilne in vort un bild*, ed. Moritz Grosman (Vilna, 1925), 52. See also Shimon Frost, *Schooling as a Socio-Political Expression* (Jerusalem: Magnes Press, 1998), 31, 38, 42.

63. Rachel Margolis, *A Partisan from Vilna*, trans. F. Jackson Piotrow (Brighton, MA: Academic Studies Press, 2010), 79–80. In the English edition of her memoirs, Margolis writes, mistakenly, that Anna Pavlovna Vygodskaia "was the wife of the prominent doctor and Jewish public figure Jakób Wygodzki," and that Anna and Jakób were the parents of the well-known Soviet Jewish writer Aleksandra Iakovlevna Brushtein. This erroneous passage did not appear in the original Russian-language edition of Margolis's memoirs, *Nemnogo sveta vo mrake: Vospominaniia* (Vil'nius: Gosudarstvennyi Evreiskii muzei imeni Vil'niusskogo Gaona, 2006), 31. Jakób was married to Elena Semënovna and not to Anna Pavlovna.

64. On feminist educational work in the interwar period, see Ellen Kellman, "Feminism and Fiction: Khane-Blankshteyn's Role in Inter-War Vilna," *Polin* 18 (2005): 221–39.

65. Yitzhak Arad, *The Holocaust in the Soviet Union* (Lincoln: University of Nebraska Press, 2009), 144–47. For a succinct overview of the Final Solution in Vil'na, see Timothy Snyder, *The Reconstruction of Nations: Poland, Ukraine, Lithuania, Belarus, 1569–1999* (New Haven: Yale University Press, 2003), 84–87.

66. Herman Kruk, *The Last Days of the Jerusalem of Lithuania: Chronicles from the Vilna Ghetto and the Camps, 1939–1944*, ed. Benjamin Harshav, trans. Barbara Harshav (New Haven: Yale University Press, 2002), 348–49.

67. Ibid., 348, n. 31.

1: Childhood Years

1. In East European Jewish society both boys and girls studied in private elementary schools (*heders*) under the direction of teachers (*melameds*), generally known for their harsh disciplinary measures and limited pedagogical abilities. The heder provided Jewish children with an education steeped in religious and cultural values but did little to prepare them for the outside world.

2. A *verst* is an obsolete unit of length used in old-regime Russia; one verst is equivalent to approximately 1.0668 kilometers.

3. In 1856, the Russian government granted Jews the right to purchase private gold mines in Siberia. By the 1870s, some of the wealthiest Jewish merchant families, including the Gintsburg family, played an active role in the development of the gold industry in Siberia. The 1897 census recorded 34,477 Jews in Siberia.

4. In Slavic folklore, Baba Yaga is a fearsome witch who flies around on a mortar or broom, kidnaps small children, and lives in a hut that stands on chicken legs.

5. Required by Jewish law to cover their hair, married Jewish women often wore bonnets of materials ranging from the modest to the more expensive, such as velvet and brocade. Wearing a wig, or *sheitel*, to cover one's own hair became increasingly popular among Jewish women in the nineteenth century.

6. In cooperation with *maskilim* (followers of the Jewish Enlightenment), the Russian government established rabbinical and teachers' seminaries in Warsaw (1826), Vil'na (1847), and Zhitomir (1847). Combining traditional Jewish learning with secular subjects, the state-sponsored seminaries admitted boys from the age of ten, who received a secondary education that lasted approximately seven years. After completing the mandatory curriculum, students studied for an additional year to receive a teacher's certificate or for an additional two years to receive a government rabbinical certificate. The seminaries produced the first generation of Jewish intellectuals who were fluent in Russian language and culture. After the Polish uprising of 1863 and the intensification of the revolutionary movement in the 1870s, the seminaries began to arouse much public controversy. In 1873, the state converted the seminaries to teacher-training institutes.

7. Avraam I. Paperna (1840–1919)—critic, educator, and proponent of the Jewish Enlightenment. After studying at the rabbinical seminary in Zhitomir (1862–64) and Vil'na (1864–67), Paperna taught in government schools, while at the same time publishing poetry, literary criticism, and Russian grammar books in Hebrew.

8. In 1840 the imperial railroad consisted of only twenty-six kilometers. After the completion of the Moscow–St. Petersburg line in 1851, Russian administrators spent large sums of money and energy on building the railroad. For the Jews of Russia, the railroad played an important role in facilitating social and geographic mobility.

9. Vygodskaia is referring to the aftermath of the Revolution of 1905, a series of uprisings and rebellions across the empire, in which workers, peasants,

students, professionals, soldiers, socialists, liberals, and ethnic minorities demand-ed political, social, and economic reform. After a general strike in fall 1905, the im-perial government issued the October Manifesto, which promised an elected leg-islative body (the duma) with far-reaching consultative powers. The government, however, dissolved the first two dumas, elected over the course of the next eighteen months. Russian Jews played a prominent role in the Revolution of 1905, and many Jewish intellectuals saw the revolutionary years (1904–7) as a major turning point for attaining full civil rights and cultural autonomy. See Abraham Ascher, *The Revo-lution of 1905*, 2 vols. (Stanford: Stanford University Press, 1988–92).

10. *Koumiss* is a mildly alcoholic drink made from fermented mare's milk, much prized by Russians and Central Asians for its curative properties.

11. A *pushke* is a small box, used predominantly as a charity or collection box.

12. To celebrate the Feast of Tabernacles, or Sukkot, East European Jews imported *esrogim* (citrons) and *lulavim* (palm fronds).

13. The *havdala* ceremony is conducted to mark the end of the holy Sab-bath, distinguishing it from the other six days of the week.

14. Seder is a ritual feast observed by Jews on the first and second nights of Passover.

15. Certain Jewish mystical traditions associate fish with prosperity and fertility.

16. *Cholent* is a traditional Jewish stew, usually with meat, potatoes, beans, and barley. *Tzimmes* is a sweetened mixture of diced vegetables and meat, of-ten with dried fruits, stewed or baked in a casserole. Because Jewish law forbids working on the Sabbath, *cholent* and *tzimmes* would be prepared the day before and left to simmer in preparation for the Sabbath meal.

17. Kugel is a baked pudding, usually made of egg noodles or potatoes.

18. Vygodskaia's recollections are not entirely correct. According to the 1897 census, Zakrochim's population consisted of 4,518 people, of whom 2,226 were Jews.

19. Published daily in St. Petersburg from 1863 to 1883, *Golos* was the preeminent Russian liberal newspaper of its day. Publication ceased by order of the imperial government of Alexander III.

20. Pliushkin is an eccentric, miserly character from Nikolai Gogol's novel *Dead Souls* (1842).

21. Similar to pinochle, sixty-six is a trick-taking card game played with a deck of twenty-four cards, and popular across Central and Eastern Europe.

22. Tens of thousands of Polish nationalists and freedom fighters were ar-rested, imprisoned, and exiled to Siberia by the imperial government following the Polish uprising of 1863–64.

23. Polish for "young lady," *panna* is often used as a form of address.

24. In Soviet Russia, where urban housing was in short supply long after the Revolution of 1917, the portmanteau phrase "living space" (*zhilploshchad'*, short for *zhilaia ploshchad'*) was used popularly to refer to any type of accommodation such as a house, apartment, or room (usually shared and usually insufficient).

25. The boy in question was likely a runaway who had been taken in by the monastery as a novitiate and baptized. Our thanks to Brian Porter-Szücs for information on Catholic monasteries in the Russian Empire.

26. Avraam I. Paperna, "Iz nikolaevskoi epokhi," *Perezhitoe* 2 (1910): 1-53; and "Detstvo i iunost," *Perezhitoe* 3 (1911): 264-364.

27. Izrael Kalmanowicz Poznanski (1833-1900)—a wealthy Jewish textile magnate, celebrated philanthropist, and financier—helped build up the financial and industrial infrastructure in Russian Poland and was a major patron of the arts and Jewish culture.

28. "*Zierlich-manierlich*" can be translated as "dainty and well-mannered."

2: Gymnasium Years

1. In Anton Chekhov's play *The Three Sisters* (1901), several characters invoke the phrase "to Moscow, to Moscow" to symbolically contrast the backward provinces with the more meaningful, culturally rich, and sophisticated life of the capital.

2. Located in the northwest region of the Russian Empire, at the confluence of the Pina and Pripet Rivers, Pinsk played an important role as a vibrant commercial and transport center. In the nineteenth century, Pinsk was also an important center of education. Jewish students attended state-sponsored elementary and government schools, vocational and social-welfare institutions, and progressive Zionist schools.

3. Ivan Davidovich Delianov served as Minister of Public Education from 1882 to 1897. Students expelled from university (on charges of radicalism or revolutionary activity, for example) could petition the ministry for readmission.

4. Dr. Abram Makover ran a children's clinic and was a prominent figure in the Jewish community of Vil'na. With Dr. Tsèmakh Shabad, he was the founder of the Vil'na branch of the Society for the Protection of the Health of the Jews (OZE), a philanthropic organization dedicated to improving health, hygiene, and sanitary conditions among impoverished Jews. Makover died of pneumonia in 1920.

5. Written by Gotthold Ephraim Lessing, *Nathan the Wise*, a dramatic play in five parts, was published in 1779. The title character is a wise Jew, unusual in eighteenth-century European literature. A plea for religious toleration, the play was read and admired by intellectuals influenced by Enlightenment thought.

6. Mark Andreevich Natanson (1850-1919) was born into a Jewish merchant family in Vil'na. While studying medicine in St. Petersburg, Natanson became active in revolutionary circles and was briefly arrested in 1869. Throughout his lifetime, Natanson continued be active in politics and was a member of the Socialist Revolutionary Party. After the February Revolution, Natanson returned to Russia; he died in Switzerland in 1919.

7. Organized along German pedagogical models, the *Realschule* was a six-year secondary school that offered students a secular curriculum focused on mathematics and science.

8. Also known as phylacteries, *tefillin* are small black boxes, usually made of leather, that contain verses from the Torah. Orthodox Jewish men strap the *tefillin* to their foreheads, arms, hands, and fingers when reciting their weekday morning prayers.

9. Reichenhall—a popular spa and resort town in the German state of Bavaria.

10. A dacha is a summer cottage, usually located in the countryside at some remove from the city.

11. Vissarion Grigor'evich Belinskii (1811–48) was an important progressive Russian literary critic and man of letters, often called the father of Russian radical intelligentsia. The son of a rural doctor, Belinskii edited two major literary magazines, *Notes of the Fatherland* and *The Contemporary*. A harsh critic of serfdom and the autocracy, Belinskii shared values and ideas that closely mirrored the Western intelligentsia. Dmitri Ivanovich Pisarev (1840–68) was a journalist, man of letters, and social critic, who is best known in the history of Russian social thought for his nihilism, defiance of order and authority, and rejection of high culture and aesthetics in favor of science and utilitarianism. Pisarev's writings were especially popular among Jewish students. Nikolai Gavrilovich Chernyshevskii (1828–89)—Russian revolutionary democrat, materialist philosopher, journalist, utopian socialist, and a leader of the revolutionary democratic movement of the 1860s. His utopian novel *What Is to Be Done?* (1863) influenced generations of student radicals.

12. Idochka's tragic fate is not recounted in these memoirs; Vygodskaia must have intended to include them in the second, uncompleted volume.

13. Cupping involves the application of heated glass cups, usually to the patient's back. The technique is supposed to draw toxins from the system and allow the patient to recuperate faster. Leeches and cupping were both popular medicinal practices across Russia and Eastern Europe. In the nineteenth century, arsenic was commonly prescribed to treat anemia, in the belief that the element aided in the body's production of red blood cells.

14. Pushkarnia (in Lithuanian, Puškornia) is a small settlement some sixty kilometers southwest of Vil'na. In Vygodskaia's day, the area was a popular destination for city dwellers who spent the summer in the scenic countryside.

15. A classic of Russian literature, *Evgenii Onegin* is a novel in verse by Aleksandr Pushkin (published in serial form between 1825 and 1832). Two of the novel's main characters are Evgenii Onegin—a Russian dandy who moves to the countryside after he inherits a country mansion—and Vladimir Lenskii, a poet whom Onegin befriends. The two men fight a duel over Lenskii's fiancée, Ol'ga Larina. Pushkin's work was the basis for Tchaikovsky's opera of the same name, which premiered in Moscow in 1879.

16. Petr Dmitrievich Boborykin (1836–1921) was a popular middlebrow Russian writer, dramatist, and man of letters. He authored twenty-six novels, over one hundred short works of fiction, and thirty plays.

17. Bel'mont, or Belmontas, is a dacha settlement outside of Vil'na, beloved by vacationers for its natural beauty.

18. By requiring all students to secure a certificate of political loyalty, the

imperial government hoped to keep radicalized young men and women from gaining access to higher education.

3: Student Years

1. The Forty Martyrs of Sebaste were subjected to a freezing death by exposure during the persecutions of the Roman emperor Licinius (r. 308–324). The Orthodox Church observes the Feast of the Forty Martyrs on March 9.

2. Once considered a fashionable district, the Petersburg Side, on the banks of the Neva River, had lost a good deal of its luster by the middle of the nineteenth century. The neighborhood encompassed a mix of residential, commercial, and industrial buildings and was home to many workers and students.

3. A celebrated historian and academician, Konstantin Nikolaevich Bestuzhev-Riumin (1829–97) was a key figure in the founding of the Higher Women's Courses. He served as first director of the Courses, which admitted its first class of students in the fall of 1878.

4. Vasil'evskii Island [Vasil'evskii Ostrov] is located across the Neva River from the Winter Palace and connected to the rest of the city by a series of bridges. Both the Women's Higher Courses and the main campus of St. Petersburg University were located there, so the district was home to many students in Vygodskaia's day. The southern embankment of Vasil'evskii Island is noted for its historic buildings, many dating to the eighteenth century, and for its rectangular grid of streets—with three main prospects running east to west and smaller "line" streets going north to south.

5. The "going to the people" movement was championed by Russian populists in the early 1870s as a way for progressive university students to bring their learning and knowledge to the Russian countryside by first educating the peasant masses and then organizing them for political action. Most Russian peasants, however, greeted their would-be pedagogues with suspicion and outright hostility. Despite its failure, the movement typified the idealism of many progressive-minded young Russian men and women of Vygodskaia's generation.

6. Dmitrii Ivanovich Mendeleev (1834–1907), internationally renowned Russian chemist famous as the "Father of the Periodic Table of Elements." Mendeleev was also active in promoting the use of scientific technology in the Russian agricultural and petroleum industries. Mendeleev's progressive political views hindered his promotion and cost him his academic career; he resigned his position at St. Petersburg University in 1890, after a bitter clash with government authorities concerning Mendeleev's support of a student petition protesting unjust conditions at the university.

7. Ivan Mikhailovich Sechenov (1829–1905), a Russian psychologist and professor at the universities of St. Petersburg, Odessa, and Moscow. Sechenov was a pioneer of neurological research in Russia and founded a physiological laboratory in St. Petersburg. Known for his discovery of evidence of localized inhibitory function in the brain, Sechenov also developed a theory that all mental

processes, innate or learned, have a physiological basis. Sechenov's mechanistic theories often brought him into conflict with imperial censors and prominent Orthodox clerics. In 1904, a year before his death, Sechenov was elected an honorary member of the Russian Academy of Sciences. Vygodskaia has confused the name of Chernyshevskii's heroine, Vera Pavlovna, with that of Sechenov's wife, Mariia Aleksandrovna Bokova-Sechenova (1839–1929), who was one of the first Russian female physicians.

8. Though suppressed by imperial censors, Nikolai Chernyshevskii's revolutionary novel *What Is to Be Done?* (1863) had an enormous impact on Russian readers, most notably the young Lenin, who borrowed the novel's title for his own political treatise of 1902. Among the protagonists of Chernyshevskii's novel are Rakhmetev and Vera Pavlovna, young people who resolve to devote themselves to the revolution and ruthlessly subordinate all aspects of their lives and beings to the cause. Chernyshevskii's "new people"—selfless, ascetic, and utterly dedicated to the perfection of society—became the prototypes for generations of self-styled Russian revolutionaries to come.

9. Nikolai Petrovich Vagner (1829–1907), Russian zoologist, entomologist, and man of letters. His fairy tales and children's stories have been described as a cross between Charles Darwin and Hans Christian Andersen. Vagner taught at St. Petersburg University from 1877 and is perhaps best noted for having discovered the phenomenon of paedogenesis, or larval reproduction.

10. Younger brother of the great Russian chemist and composer Alexander Borodin, the botanist and academician Ivan Parfen'evich Borodin (1847–1930) enjoyed a celebrated career that spanned the late imperial and early Soviet periods. I. P. Borodin was the founder and first president of the Russian Botanical Society, and one of the leading pioneers in the Russian conservation movement. He served as vice president of the Russian Academy of Sciences from 1917 to 1919.

11. Aleksandr Aleksandrovich Inostrantsev (1843–1919), geologist and professor at St. Petersburg University from 1873, where he founded a geological laboratory and museum. Inostrantsev was famed for his fieldwork in northern Russia and was the author of a university textbook on geology that went through multiple editions in the early twentieth century. The spa that Vygodskaia mentions is located in present-day Lithuania (Druskininkai).

12. Aleksandr Mikhailovich Butlerov (1828–86), professor of chemistry at St. Petersburg University from 1868 to 1885. Butlerov was most famous for his theory of chemical structure, which influenced organic chemists for generations to come. Outside of the laboratory, Butlerov was best known for his belief in science as a tool for cultural progress and the advancement of society. A proponent of educational reform, Butlerov was a champion of women's higher education and the Bestuzhev Courses.

13. Orest Fedorovich Miller (1833–89) graduated from Moscow University in 1855 and afterward taught at St. Petersburg University until his death. He was a specialist in Russian epic poetry and wrote his doctoral thesis on the legend of Il'ia Muromets. Miller was among the most talented exponents of the so-called mythological school, which held that epic poetry was a reflection of folk consciousness.

14. Nikolai Ivanovich Kareev (1850–1931), philosopher, ethicist, and historian, taught at the universities of Warsaw and St. Petersburg and was elected a corresponding member of the Soviet Academy of Sciences in 1929. Kareev was a political moderate, but greatly influenced by more radical thinkers such as Aleksandr Herzen, Dmitrii Pisarev, and Petr Lavrov. Kareev stressed the dignity and worth of the individual and criticized philosophical attempts to reduce men and women to the level of mere social organisms.

15. Ivan Ivanovich Borgman (1849–1914), prominent physicist and authority on electricity and magnetism. Borgman served as the first elected rector of St. Petersburg University (1905–10).

16. Nikolai Aleksandrovich Gezekhus (1845–1919) was a Russian physicist best known for his research on the so-called spheroidal state of liquids. From 1889 until 1918, he served as rector of the Petersburg Technological Institute.

17. Nadezhda Vasil'evna Stasova (1822–95) was born to a noble family at Tsarskoe Selo, outside the imperial capital. The daughter of a court architect to Alexander I, and the goddaughter of the tsar himself, Stasova dedicated her adult life to philanthropic causes and social reform, working to provide clean and sanitary housing for poor women in St. Petersburg, establishing shelters and reading circles to rehabilitate prostitutes and other "fallen women," and founding a women's publishing cooperative. As director of the Bestuzhev Courses, Stasova was one of the most prominent voices calling for women's right to higher education.

18. By the middle of the nineteenth century, the word *zhid* had become a common term of disparagement to describe a Jew. See John D. Klier, "*Zhid*: The Biography of a Russian Pejorative," *Slavonic and East European Review* 60, no. 1 (1982): 1–15.

19. To put these figures in some perspective, a single woman worker in St. Petersburg in the early twentieth century earned approximately twenty-four rubles a month. See Rose L. Glickman, *Russian Factory Women: Workplace and Society, 1880–1914* (Berkeley and Los Angeles: University of California Press, 1984), 115.

20. A *kalach* is a baked loaf, often braided, popular in Russian and Slavic cuisine.

21. Meshchanskaia Street is located near the notorious Haymarket, a seedy site made famous in Dostoevsky's *Crime and Punishment*. The district was home to many prostitutes, and Vygodskaia's intimations suggest that her landlady's "daughter" may have been one of them.

22. Born to a noble family, Mikhail Evgrafovich Saltykov-Shchedrin (1826–89) was educated at the Alexander Lycée in St. Petersburg and embarked upon a civil service career in the War Ministry. He published his first short stories in 1847–48; deemed subversive by the censors, these early works earned him exile to Viatka. Beginning in 1856, Saltykov-Shchedrin was a frequent contributor to some of the most prominent Petersburg literary journals. After official pressure to resign his civil service post, Saltykov-Shchedrin devoted himself full time to literary pursuits and became principal editor of *Otechestvennye Zapiski* (Notes from the Fatherland) after the death of Nikolai Nekrasov in 1878.

Saltykov-Shchedrin's work often satirized the Russian state bureaucracy as corrupt, inefficient, and arbitrary.

23. Founded in 1863 by Evzel' Gintsburg, the Society for the Promotion of Enlightenment among the Jews of Russia became the leading Jewish voluntary organization in the empire. Designed to remake Jews into more economically useful and culturally integrated subjects, the society provided scholarships and grants, encouraged Jews to learn Russian, and attempted to create a network of modern schools for adults. The society remained active until 1929. The friend to whom Vygodskaia refers here is likely P. P. Antokol'skaia, who became a prominent Jewish educator in St. Petersburg.

24. Semën Iakovlevich Nadson (1862-87) was one of the most popular and widely published poets in late imperial Russia. Nadson's poetry portrayed the 1880s in Russia as a tarnished age of materialism and vulgar consumerism. Young readers, in particular, were responsive to the themes of idealism, loss, and melancholy explored in Nadson's poetry.

25. Born to a Jewish farming family in the south of Ukraine, Semën Grigor'evich Frug (1860-1916) was among the first to tackle Jewish themes in Russian verse; later in life, he switched to writing in Yiddish. Frug's lyric poetry was often set to music and became very popular on the late imperial stage.

26. Regarded as one of the founding fathers of Russian modernism, Nikolai Maksimovich Minskii (1855-1937) was an eclectic writer and thinker whose works ranged from poetry to aesthetics. Minskii also wrote revolutionary verse and a few plays. He was arrested by the imperial police for his work on an underground Bolshevik newspaper and forced to emigrate. He spent the remainder of his life in Western Europe; he died in Paris in 1937.

27. Afanasii Afanas'evich Fet (1820-92) was one of the leading figures in the movement known as "Art for Art's Sake." His first collection of verses, entitled *Liricheskii panteon* (The Lyrical Pantheon), appeared in 1840. His poetry was noted for its musicality and lyricism, but Fet's deliberate lack of engagement with social and political questions of the day elicited criticism from some contemporaries.

28. Mikhail Mikhailovich Koriakin (1850-97), a celebrated Russian bass who achieved his greatest fame on the Petersburg stage. Koriakin's operatic repertoire included thirty-eight roles, most notably that of Ivan Susanin in Glinka's *A Life for the Tsar.*

29. Evgeniia Konstantinovna Mravina (1864-1914), a Russian soprano and principal soloist at the Mariinskii Theater, renowned for her strong acting ability and the purity of her tone.

30. Nicknamed "The Enchantress of the Russian Stage," Mariia Gavrilovna Savina (1854-1915) headlined at the Aleksandrinskii Theater in Petersburg for more than forty years. A great favorite of the novelist Ivan Turgenev, Savina was a fierce rival of the actress Strepetova.

31. A popular tragic actress known for her realistic acting style, Polina Antip'evna Strepetova (1850-1903) and the strong characters she portrayed were beloved by Slavophiles, populists, and proponents of women's emancipation alike.

32. Kvass is a popular Russian beverage made from fermented black or rye bread.

33. Oral examinations in imperial Russia emphasized rote memorization over critical thought. The student would draw the required number of cards or chits and answer the question that was printed on the back. In the variation that Vygodskaia describes, the cards were numbered, each corresponding to a specific exam question.

34. Vygodskaia is probably referring to Cross Island [Krestovskii Ostrov], the largest of the islands located in the Neva delta, north of the Petersburg Side. In the nineteenth century, this was a popular recreation site for the working class of the imperial capital.

35. "Between you and me."

36. "Madame, I must tell you, the little one is charming, simply charming!"

37. Vygodskaia appears to be quoting from a well-known fable set to verse by the Russian scholar and man of letters Mikhail Vasil'evich Lomonosov (1711-65).

38. Vygodskaia is referring to the estate at Markuciai, where Pushkin's son Grigorii lived with his wife, Varvara, between 1899 and 1905.

39. Aleksandr Nikolaevich Ostrovskii (1823-86) was one of the most popular Russian playwrights of the nineteenth century. His early plays *A Family Affair* and *The Bankrupt* were known for their scathingly satirical depictions of provincial life and the Russian merchant classes.

40. Vygodskaia refers to a pair of three-handed card games very popular in nineteenth-century Russia.

41. Now known as Tartu, Dorpat is in southern Estonia. The city's famed university was founded in 1802 by order of Emperor Alexander I.

42. A lieutenant in the Russian navy, Nikolai Nikolaevich Figner (1857-1918) retired from a promising military career in 1881 to study at the St. Petersburg Conservatory. He toured Europe and South America and was the lead tenor at the Mariinskii Theater until 1903.

43. Vygodskaia is likely referring to Konstantin Mikhailov-Stoian (1853-1914), a well-known Bulgarian tenor who performed and directed across the Russian Empire.

44. The Italian-born Medea Figner (1859-1952) was the second wife of Nikolai Figner (the couple divorced in 1904) and headlined as the star soprano of the Mariinskii Theater from 1887 to 1912. Medea Figner starred opposite her husband in the Petersburg premiere of Tchaikovsky's opera *The Queen of Spades*, in December 1890.

45. Fyodor Ignat'evich Stravinskii (1843-1902) was a celebrated Russian bass. Best known for his portrayal of Mephistopheles in Gounod's *Faust*, Stravinskii made 1,235 appearances in sixty-four operatic roles. Father of the famed Russian composer Igor Stravinskii.

46. Born in 1864, Ol'ga Ol'gina was a soloist at the Mariinskii Theater in the 1890s. A soprano, she played the lead female role in the premiere performance of Borodin's *Prince Igor* in 1890.

47. Angelo Masini (1844-1926), an Italian tenor, much admired by Chaliapin. Verdi described Masini's voice as "the most divine I have ever heard." Serov's portrait of Masini hangs in the Tretyakov Gallery in Moscow.

48. Vygodskaia may refer here to Salvatore Cottone, an Italian baritone and pianist, who accompanied tenor Enrico Caruso in his historic recordings of 1902-4.

49. In his prime, in the last decades of the nineteenth century, Jean de Reszke (1850-1925) was perhaps the most renowned operatic tenor in the world. He often performed alongside his brother, Edouard (1853-1917), a famous bass.

50. Dame Nellie Melba (1861-1931), an Australian soprano who enjoyed international acclaim for her high range and coloratura skills. She performed in Russia in 1891, by special invitation of Alexander III.

51. Virginia Ferni-Germano (1849-1934), an Italian soprano and violinist who appeared onstage across Europe.

52. Vera Nikolaevna Figner (1852-1942) was a member of the executive committee of the People's Will, a radical movement dedicated to the overthrow of the autocracy. She participated in organizing the assassination of Alexander II in 1881. Arrested in 1883, Figner spent twenty years imprisoned at the Schlüsselburg fortress.

53. Vygodskaia is referring to a pivotal scene in act III of *Otello* by the Italian composer Giuseppe Verdi. Based on Shakespeare's tragic play, Verdi's opera made its Russian premiere at the Mariinskii in 1887, with Nikolai Figner in the title role.

54. The son of Russian peasants, Fyodor Ivanovich Chaliapin (1873-1938) was the most famous bass of his day and an international celebrity. He emigrated from Soviet Russia in 1921 and spent the remainder of his life and career in the West. Perhaps best known for his portrayal of the title role in Modest Mussorgsky's *Boris Godunov*, Chaliapin also sang the role of the miller in Aleksandr Sergeevich Dargomyzhskii's 1856 opera, *Rusalka*, based on a poem by Pushkin.

55. *Evgenii Onegin*, book VIII, stanza 29. Vygodskaia here has substituted "music" for Pushkin's "love."

56. Based on *La dame aux camélias* by Alexandre Dumas, *La Traviata* (1853) is perhaps Verdi's most popular opera. It was performed regularly by Russian companies in Moscow and St. Petersburg in Vygodskaia's day.

57. Born in Krakow, the pianist Józef Kazimierz Hofmann (1876-1957) first made his reputation touring the European continent and the United States as a child prodigy in the 1880s.

58. Famed for his technique and the richness of his tone, Anton Grigor'evich Rubinstein (1829-1894) was the greatest Russian pianist of the nineteenth century. The son of a Jewish family who had converted to Russian Orthodoxy, Rubinstein achieved international fame. As the founder and first director of the St. Petersburg Conservatory, Rubinstein had an enormous influence on Russian musicians in his day.

59. Born in Moscow and educated in Germany and Sweden, Sof'ia Vasil'evna Kovalevskaia (1850-91) became the first woman in Europe to earn

a doctorate in mathematics. In 1889, Kovalevskaia was awarded a tenured professorship at the University of Stockholm, making her the first woman on the continent to hold a university professorship. She died of pneumonia at the age of forty-one. Vygodskaia is mistaken in stating that Kovalevskaia graduated from the Bestuzhev Courses. She played a key role in the founding of the Courses but, because of her past brushes with radicalism, was not permitted to teach there. Our thanks to Barbara Alpern Engel for establishing this connection.

60. Dr. Tsèmakh Shabad (1864-1935) was a prominent physician, folklorist, and philanthropist, and the founder of the Vil'na branch of YIVO. Shabad was an acquaintance of the Russian writer Kornei Chukovskii, who based the popular character of Dr. Aibolit (Dr. Ouch It Hurts), hero of his most famous children's story, on him.

61. *The Madcap* (*Sorvanets*) is an 1888 comedy in three acts by the prolific and popular Russian playwright Viktor Aleksandrovich Krylov (1838-1906).

62. The *smotrina* was a traditional Russian wedding custom in which the groom's family came to the bride's home to look her over and inspect her.

63. Lucius Licinius Lucullus was a patrician of the Roman Republic, famous for his bountiful feasts and extravagant gastronomical tastes.

64. Petr Frantsevich Lesgaft (1837-1909), a celebrated anatomist and pedagogue; acknowledged as the father of physical education training in Russia.

65. Nikolai Aleksandrovich Dobroliubov (1836-61) wrote for the journal *Sovremennik* (The Contemporary) and was the most celebrated radical critic of his day. His most famous article, "What Is Oblomovism?" (1859), excoriated educated Russian society for its inactivity and indolence. Vygodskaia appears to have confused the timing of the demonstrations, which took place on November 17, 1886.

66. "Eternal Memory" (*Vechnaia pamiat'*) is a chant traditionally sung at the close of a Russian Orthodox funeral service.

67. A notorious reactionary and antisemite, Lieutenant-General Petr Apollonovich Gresser (1833-92) served as chief of police in Petersburg from 1882 to 1883. From 1883 until his death he was head of the city administration in the capital.

68. Born in modern-day Latvia, and a graduate of the University of Dorpat, Woldemar Kernig (1840-1917) was a pioneer in the field of neurophysics, best known for his work in diagnosing meningitis. From 1890 he was chief physician at the Obukhov Women's Hospital in St. Petersburg.

69. August Rauber (1841-1917) was head of the Institute of Anatomy, Histology, and Embryology at Dorpat for nearly thirty years. Physiologist K. E. Shmidt (1822-94) studied the chemical composition of gastric acid.

70. The preeminent Russian gynecologist of his day, and author of some 150 scholarly works, Dmitrii Oskarovich Otto (1855-1929) was a renowned pedagogue and a champion of equal rights for female physicians. From 1899 he served as director of the Women's Medical Institute in St. Petersburg.

71. The site had been a popular commercial center for market stalls in Petersburg since the late eighteenth century. By Vygodskaia's time, the Apraksin

market had grown into a large shopping complex of several dozen stores, located near the Fontanka River.

72. *The Bird Seller* (1891) was a popular comic operetta in three acts by the Austrian composer Carl Zeller.

73. Younger sister of the great playwright Ostrovskii, Nadezhda Niko-laevna Ostrovskaia (1842–1918) achieved modest fame in her own right as a pedagogue and writer. Her children's stories drew on experiences from her own childhood spent at the family estate in Shchelykovo, while subtly calling into question such institutions as autocracy, religion, and the social hierarchy. In the 1870s and 1880s, Ostrovskaia was actively engaged in promoting the cause of women's education and organizing philanthropic charities for young governesses and educators.

74. Vygodskaia appears to have mistaken the date. The Exposition Universelle was an international exhibition of arts, crafts, and industrial wonders held in Paris in 1889 to coincide with the centenary of the French Revolution. The exhibition attracted more than thirty-two million visitors from around the world.

75. Mikhail Evgrafovich Saltykov-Shchedrin (see n. 22, above).

4: Between School and Life

1. From the Russian for "trio," a troika is a Russian sleigh or carriage drawn by a team of three horses.

2. Vygodskaia's right to reside in the capital would have expired following her completion of the Courses.

3. Founded by a German immigrant in 1818, the Schröder company was the preeminent manufacturer of pianos in the Russian capital.

4. The Russo-Turkish War (1877–78) saw Russia supporting the nationalist independence movements of Orthodox Christian Slavic peoples against Ottoman rule. As per the Treaty of San Stefano and the Congress of Berlin (1878), the Ottoman Empire recognized the independence of Romania, Serbia, and Montenegro, and the autonomy of Bulgaria.

5. Small, knotted pastries boiled in a sweet honey syrup, and a preserved fruit spread, respectively.

6. Vygodskaia does not specify what that purpose was, though we might surmise that the jewels were sold to pay for her travel and tuition abroad.

7. Jewish tradition says that joy is multiplied during the Hebrew month of Adar (March–April), so many consider this an opportune time to marry. The phrase "God saw that it was good" appears twice on the third day of the creation story, and thus many Jews believe Tuesday (the third day of the Jewish week) an auspicious day to perform a wedding ceremony.

8. Merchants in imperial Russia were divided into categories, or guilds, based on the value of their assets. In 1859, Jewish merchants of the first guild, the highest rank, were granted the right to settle permanently outside the Pale of Settlement.

9. To put Vygodskaia's figures in some perspective, a female worker in a Moscow tailor shop in the 1910s could expect to earn about 277 rubles a year. See E. A. Oliunina, "The Tailoring Trade in Moscow and the Villages of Moscow and Riazan Provinces: Material on the History of the Domestic Industry in Russia," in Victoria E. Bonnell, *The Russian Worker: Life and Labor under the Tsarist Regime* (Berkeley: University of California Press, 1983), 166.

10. Vygodskaia is referring to the *chuppah*. Meant to symbolize the home that the couple will build together, the chuppah is a canopy under which the bride and groom stand during a Jewish wedding ceremony.

11. An *arshin* is an old Russian unit of measure, equivalent to 0.71 meters.

Index

www.ingramcontent.com/pod-product-compliance
Ingram Content Group UK Ltd.
Pitfield, Milton Keynes, MK11 3LW, UK
UKHW042149060225
454777UK00004B/405